MASTERING THE AUDITION

HOW TO PERFORM UNDER PRESSURE

By Donna Soto-Morettini

D1328750

Methuen Drama

To Martin Lowe and Joel Fram,
who began this journey with me

CONTENTS

MASTE ON

HOW TO PERFORM UNDER PRESSURE

Published by Methuen Drama 2012

Methuen Drama, an imprint of Bloomsbury Publishing Plc

1 3 5 7 9 10 8 6 4 2

Methuen Drama
Bloomsbury Publishing Plc
50 Bedford Square
London WC1B 3DP
www.methuendrama.com

Copyright © Donna Soto-Morettini 2012

Donna Soto-Morettini has asserted her rights under the Copyright, Designs and Patents Act 1988 to be identified as the author of this work

ISBN: 978 1 408 16061 9

A CIP catalogue record for this book is available from the British Library

Available in the USA from Bloomsbury Academic & Professional,
175 Fifth Avenue/3rd Floor, New York, NY 10010

Typeset by Mark Heslington Ltd, Scarborough, North Yorkshire
Printed and bound in the UK by MPG Books Ltd, Bodmin, Cornwall

ACKNOWLEDGEMENTS

Deep and heartfelt thanks go to Sian Beilock, David Grindrod, Trevor Jackson, Ellen Lewis and Jason Selk for so kindly allowing me to interview them for this book.

To the many kind volunteer artists who contributed in so many ways to this book, my deep thanks for your time and your honesty: Lena Aarstad, Ashley Alymann, Kate Barker, Amy Booth-Steel, Erin Breen, Shaun Carlin, Dai Crisp, Thomas Cunningham, Antonia Davies, Josh Finkel, Katie Foster, Joel Fram, Nora Gombos, Hannah Hammond, Petra Karr, Dermot Keaney, Daniel Langley, Andrew Langtree, Martin Lowe, Duncan MacInnes, Abigail McKern, Jay McWinen, Sarah Middleton, Andrea Minns, David Morrell, Jon Nathan, Jason Nicholls-Carrer, Johanne Noble, Kelly Jo O'Leary, Lise Olson, Roxaneh Renton, Jennifer Rhodes, Oliver Roll, Neil Simpson, Gavin Spokes, Lisa Stokke, Natalie Toyne, Emma Vaudrey, Bart Williams.

Sian Beilock is a leading expert on cognitive science and on the many factors influencing all types of performance. She is an Associate Professor in the Department of Psychology at the University of Chicago, and her book *Choke: What the Secrets of the Brain Reveal about Getting It Right When You Have to* was published by Free Press (Simon & Schuster) in 2010.

David Grindrod's UK casting includes *Chicago, Mamma Mia!, Matilda, Ghost, The Wizard of Oz, Sister Act, Shrek, West Side Story, How to Train Your Dragon* and *Viva Forever*. Film casting includes Ensemble for *Mamma Mia!*, UK Dancers for *Nine* and *The Phantom of the Opera*. TV includes *How Do You Solve a Problem Like Maria?, Any Dream Will Do, I'd Do Anything, Over the Rainbow* and *Superstar*. David Grindrod Associates is a member of the Casting Directors' Guild of Great Britain.

Trevor Jackson is Executive Producer and Head of Casting for Cameron Mackintosh. He trained at the Webber Douglas Academy and has been involved in casting musicals for almost thirty years both for Cameron Mackintosh and previously for Andrew Lloyd Webber's Really Useful Group. Casting credits include *Miss Saigon, Cats, Phantom of the Opera, Mary Poppins, Betty Blue Eyes* and *Les Misérables*.

Ellen Lewis worked for Juliet Taylor before becoming one of the most successful independent casting directors in New York. She has cast films for Martin Scorsese, Mike Nichols, Jim Jarmusch, Stanley Tucci and other notable directors. Her film credits include: *Forrest Gump, Gangs of New York, Angels in America, The Aviator, The Devil Wears Prada, The Departed, Hugo, Extremely Loud and Incredibly Close* and *Boardwalk Empire*.

Dr Jason Selk LPC, NCC is the Director of Mental Training for the St Louis Cardinals and best-selling author of *10-Minute Toughness* and *Executive Toughness*. Jason is a regular contributor to ABC, CBS, ESPN and NBC radio and television and has been featured in *USA Today, Men's Health, Muscle and Fitness, Shape* and *Self* magazines. Jason utilizes his in-depth knowledge and experience of working with the world's finest athletes, coaches and business leaders to help individuals and organisations outperform their competition.

PART 1:
THE AUDITIONING MIND

1 INTRODUCTION

This book is divided into two sections, the first descriptive and the second practical. They add up to a truly unique way of looking at the whole process of auditioning. This first section of the book is about situating the audition process within the context of contemporary research into how we function under pressure. Drawing on areas like neuroscience and psychology, it will help you get closer to understanding what the real obstacles are in your quest to master auditions, and it will provide the basis for the second 'Toolkit' section.

Chasing 'it'

The last girl comes in at about 7:30. She looks good, although the panel is aware that there are already more longhaired brunettes than needed on the callback list. She sings little bits of three different songs and she is fine. Good pitch. Pleasant tone. Some imagination in the delivery. The Executive Producer says 'Tell me a little bit about yourself' and the girl rattles on a bit about how much she has always loved performing and how important this part is to her. She talks about playing a similar part and how wonderful the experience was. As she walks out of the room there is the kind of silence that always follows this kind of audition. What to do with this one? She might be filed under the (deadly) category: useful. She might be (deadlier still) rejected. She might be asked back in because, after spending nearly ten minutes with her, for some reason people still haven't really got a clue who she is. The question of course, is: What are the panel looking for? They might answer that by saying that there is no preconceived 'ideal' here, and that they'll know what they want when the right person walks in the door. Or they might admit that as the day wears on, they are desperate to take an easy route and just want someone to walk through the door who will solve the casting problem for them. Or they might be very astute, and admit that probably every person behind the table is looking for something slightly different. But even if they agree on the truth of the last answer, they still have a problem. What to do with this girl?

I think the hardest moment of auditioning is this one, because it's the moment when everyone is lost. The poor girl who just auditioned is lost, because her dream job has just slipped through her fingers. The panel is lost because they can only look at each other and say ineffectual things like 'I don't know' and hope that someone in the room has a strong feeling somewhere that they can latch onto. These are the moments when everyone is grateful for that single confident voice that says something like 'there's just no wow factor here' or 'that just didn't do it for me'. Everyone – and I mean everyone – knows how inadequate this language is, but at the same time, everyone has to agree. They know that they just saw a pleasant and competent audition that didn't have 'it', but although they're pretty sure they know 'it' when they see it, they can't seem to adequately define what 'it' is when they're asked. They're looking for 'it', they're in the business of trying to find 'it' but even though the great majority of time behind that mysterious audition table is devoted to chasing and securing 'it', could they ever actually articulate what 'it' is?

Of course, audition panels are not alone in looking for 'it'. The people who audition – for amateur productions or professional; for West End shows or reality television; for straight drama or musical theatre; for drama school or agency representation – are also trying to find 'it' in their own performances and finding themselves similarly ineffectual at defining just what 'it' might be. Sometimes the auditioning person *knows* that they don't have 'it' but that they may be quite good as company or ensemble members or just useful understudy types. But generally people auditioning are simply perplexed by the fact that they aren't being successful and perhaps they wonder if the problem is that they just don't have 'it'.

We've become addicted to watching auditions – either in the form of reality dance/song show contestants 'auditioning' for your home vote, or in the early episodes of shows like *The X Factor*, *Britain's Got Talent* or *American Idol*, which are devoted entirely to the auditioning process. But could any of us ever define the elusive 'it' we're looking for or believe we've found when we pick up the phone to vote for our favourite singer/dancer?

The girl I described above has done everything right. She's been to drama school, worked hard, was considered one of the best in her class. She's read all the books on how to audition and tried to take on their advice. She has a portfolio of pretty good material ready to present when asked. She's pleasant and open minded in the interview and has a few interesting things to say about herself and the last part she played. She's dressed suitably for this casting and she looks nice on screen. She's done some professional work since leaving drama school – a good role in a Panto and a chorus/swing part in a sadly short-run musical. She wants this role, clearly, she's reasonably well-suited to it and would no doubt work hard if cast. But somehow there's no spark. *She just doesn't have 'it'.*

So here we are – all of us chasing 'it' but not able to talk about what 'it' might be. Could it be confidence? Uniqueness? A 'look'? A 'sound'? A point of view? Something related to all of these things?

But before we answer that, can we even agree that 'it' exists? Surely the more you talk to casting directors (and the more you serve as one) the more you begin to wonder if 'it' actually exists, or whether 'it' is just a kind of shorthand way of excusing our own personal preferences/prejudices when we're offering a part or a place. When we see someone who doesn't match up to the ideal we had in our heads about the role before coming into the room – and whatever they might say, most directors do have that pre-audition 'ideal' in their heads – do we just say that this or that person just didn't have that 'it' factor, and hope that we won't have to explain further?

That might be possible. And it might even explain why the people behind the table so often disagree on what they've just seen. But it wouldn't explain those moments (and believe me, there are many) when all the people behind the table give a collective sigh of relief – or maybe that's a muted 'whoop' of excitement – and suddenly agree that the last candidate had 'it'. Surely this proves that we can collectively recognise 'it' when we see it and if that's true, then 'it' cannot just be each panel member's individual preferences or prejudices. But when that collective panel 'eureka' moment doesn't happen, then we're left with questions about how and why we make audition decisions. In cases like the one above, the question is often solved by the 'Randy, yes or no?' form of panel democracy. Although a single strong vote from any one department (choreographer, MD, director) can often outweigh two tentative 'yes' votes, so the democracy is tempered by . . . well . . . temper.

Tales from the Land of Oz

The idea for this book has been slowly germinating since the very first Andrew Lloyd Webber show, *How Do You Solve a Problem Like Maria?*, for which I worked as casting director. I've done five subsequent nation-wide tours as a casting director – *Any Dream Will Do*, *I'd Do Anything*, *Over the Rainbow*, *Superstar* and *The Voice* – so I hope you'll forgive a little detour here, as so much of what inspired this book has come from these combined experiences.

The shows are compelling viewing for many because they seem to combine the right ingredients for our age – agony, ecstasy, surprising amateurs and life-changing results. These components seem to fuel the most successful television these days from *Deal or No Deal* to *MasterChef*. The ever-fascinating part for me comes in the national rounds of auditions, during which we see many thousands of people. It's a bit like taking the collective performing arts temperature of the country. And it is an interesting clash of cultures. Some of the best and brightest casting directors in the country get involved in this, yet most of the people we see are not professional and many have never trained. So the auditions we see for these shows are miles away from the professional circumstances that most of the casting directors working on them are used to.

We see an interesting cross-section of people, and not only do these rather extraordinary experiences open up the question of how an audition works, they also open up the question of *why* people audition, and what purpose auditioning plays in people's lives. I've learned that auditions are pretty deeply entwined with our sense of risk, validation, exploration and, indeed, *who* we are.

Reality casting auditions are similar to any other open-call audition – and that usually means that people disregard the normal constraints: we routinely see people of the wrong age and type audition for the roles of Maria, Joseph, Nancy and Dorothy, although for *The Voice* we were gloriously free from such constraints. But what does it mean to talk about the *right* type for a role? That question is more fraught than you might think, and working on the Andrew Lloyd Webber shows has been an interesting education in the subject. I say this because it's relatively common to think of the person auditioning as the 'dreamer' in the room. They are dreaming of their 'ideal' role and hoping to do their 'ideal' performance in the quest to get that role. They're also engaged in a whole lot of other things like trying to be fearless in the face of what is generally agreed to be a pretty terrifying experience, and wanting to prove that (if only to themselves perhaps) they really *can* do what they think they can do. In essence, they're looking for something to validate their dreams and auditioning is the rock face of 'reality'. But I often find myself wondering who the real dreamer in the room is. When we talk about the 'right type' for a role we are in some very shifting terrain, because in my experience the *real* dreamers in the room are sitting *behind* the audition table.

This has something to do with the different ways in which casting directors take on a set of auditions. Some casting people approach a project with an open mind. That means that they're sometimes willing to work very hard with someone who might have a 'look' or a certain quality about them, even if they're not quite hitting all the requirements for a role. These people will often spend much time trying to bring things out in an auditionee which may, in fact, just not be there.

But some casting people approach a project with a very set idea in mind, and for these folk even performers who are a close but not quite exact fit for their 'ideal' may get short shrift. In either case, the casting director, musical director, choreographer, director or producer involved is probably pursuing their own dream of how they see the role played and by whom. The problem for the auditioning performer is that, as often as not, the casting team sitting behind the table may be having different dreams.

But that's only one of the tough things about the audition process. The fact is, the whole of the process is pretty unreliable. A brief tale from *Over the Rainbow* illustrates this fact pretty neatly, I think. Our first work with the girls took place at 'Dorothy Farm' (this was the name we had for the intensive training part of *Over the Rainbow*). The Farm was out in the wilds of Hertfordshire somewhere, and we all arrived one freezing cold morning in February. If you've never seen one of these shows, the journey goes something like this: we travel to cities around the UK seeing auditionees in 'filter rooms' first. This is the first contact between candidate and casting person, and the great majority of those auditioning are, as the name suggests, filtered out at this stage. A small percentage are 'put through' to the casting room where a decision is made as to whether the candidate should be sent through to a London recall. About 100 candidates are sent to the recalls, and some fifty more are eliminated until we end up with a final fifty for 'Nancy School' or 'Dorothy Farm'. However, once we arrived I was taken aside by the Series Editor, who explained that the fifty girls had a bit of a surprise in store. The casting panel had had a 'sleepless night' over a few of their decisions and as a result had decided that four of the girls they'd let go in London should actually have been given the chance to go through to the intensive training stage. It fell to me to announce this wonderful surprise to the fifty waiting hopefuls. I'll be honest, it wasn't a job I relished. Why on earth would fifty anxious girls welcome four more competitors into their midst? But even more worrying to me was *why*, when we had already whittled some 10,000 down to fifty – out of which we could only choose twenty – should we be taking on four more (clearly) borderline cases? We already had more than enough girls to consider, I thought, so what was the point in bringing back four girls who would most likely end up being sent right back home at the end of our three-day intensive on the farm?

In the end, this last-minute change of heart on the part of the judges proved to be a very interesting – if unintended – experiment in the accuracy of judgement in the audition situation. Against what would seem to be pretty impossible odds, not only did three out of the four 'borderline' girls make it into the final 20, but two out of the four made it into the final five on the live shows! Of course, the only conclusion I can reach about this doggedly unscientific study is that auditioning, as a process, must be a pretty hopeless thing. Because if two girls who were consigned to the audition scrapheap one day somehow managed to make it to the top five out of some 10,000 other contestants, you have to wonder what it was that the original panel missed and who else might wrongly have been 'weeded' out.

The imprecise nature of the audition process shouldn't be too surprising to anyone, as most people who do them – whichever side of the table they're on – are quick to admit that it's a flawed but necessary process. Most experienced auditioners know how little of their true capability can be seen in an audition. But what makes the Andrew Lloyd Webber shows interesting is that we get to test that proposition – and not only in this early situation.

Getting Over the Rainbow

Can we learn anything at all from this manufactured kind of audition? The answer I think is a resounding yes – but we're probably not learning what we think we are. In *Over the Rainbow*, for example, despite the fact that the entire show is ostensibly geared toward trying to find a Dorothy, we really didn't have time to look for a Dorothy. That would have required a whole lot of things we couldn't get around to – like seeing how the potential Dorothy worked with the other members of the cast, testing the sound of the voice on the new material being written for the show, working on extended sections of the script under direction, etc. As we couldn't really test any of this, what we were really testing was something else entirely: stamina, courage, flexibility and the ability to learn quickly under tremendous pressure. Most audition systems don't have the capacity to test for this. Most auditions involve looking very directly at what a part needs and what a candidate brings at that moment. In other words, they look for a direct match between role and abilities displayed. The Andrew Lloyd Webber television audition shows work in a far more oblique way, but given the success of each of the people who've won the roles (and the many further successes of those who have battled their way into the top ten or twelve), perhaps there's really something significant to consider in this oblique approach?

Just surviving the demands of these reality shows for ten weeks would challenge the toughest professional. Any performer who makes it to the final weeks has simply proven a kind of stamina – both physical and mental – that few of us would imagine that we possess. They also demonstrate a surprising ability to learn a great deal of material under pressure, and as the shows go on, that ability increases slightly over each week.

Of course, courage is a major factor. Picking yourself up off the floor after you've been publicly flattened by one of the guest judges and then facing immediate 'how-did-that-make-you-feel' camera interviews requires a stout heart. Having only half-an-hour or so to pull yourself together and then smile through the opening number of the 'results' show (all while the prospect of being unceremoniously booted off the show through the humiliation of a public vote must be looming in the mind) demands some real audacity.

Finally, the prospect of being given a huge amount of material to learn each week (with no time to research or properly prepare), having the challenge of getting through and retaining a pretty daunting set of lyrics and choreographic routines, and then being able to take on-the-spot direction that will hopefully add some depth to all the time-frenzied superficiality of this kind of performance really demands a kind of mental flexibility that few seasoned performers have. In essence, these shows seriously test their candidates. But they test something in an exhaustive way that we could never test in a standard audition format.

Of course, it isn't cost effective to audition by producing a lavish Saturday night TV show, but doesn't all this raise some questions that are worth considering for an auditioning performer and an audition panel? And aren't the most critical questions related to whether we are seeking the right things when we audition and whether – in that search – it is better to be testing directly or indirectly for a role? In other words, most panels are keen to actually go through all of the materials (songs, scenes) exhaustively and listen to and watch the candidate in the direct circumstances that the play would put them into. But might it be just as valid (or perhaps even wiser) to go the indirect route? Might these shows demonstrate the virtue of taking the oblique approach (once the basics are covered: yes, the voice is up to it, the 'look' is okay, etc.) and testing other things like flexibility and willingness to risk or to do more than would seem reasonable? For the auditioning performer, perhaps the critical questions lie in just how important the 'oblique' qualities (such as courage, stamina, flexibility and the ability to learn under tremendous pressure) might be, and whether – along with all the other things we study in preparation for a performance career – these things might matter as much as talent? Could these qualities give us a kind of extraordinary confidence that just might read as that 'it' factor?

I don't have the definitive answer to any of those questions, but having been part of casting teams for many years, they niggle away at me. As does the entire question of what auditions are, what they really mean to us, and how we might be better as we go about them. And while I've come to suspect that, along with great talent, evidence of the 'oblique' abilities mentioned above might be a part of that elusive 'it' factor, I'm aware that training in courage, stamina and flexibility isn't part of the standard drama-school curriculum. In fact, I think these are things we have to acquire for ourselves. Part of what I'm hoping to do in this book is to set out some strategies to help you do just that.

As you may have gathered by now, this book is an attempt to do something really different from the usual 'tips and techniques' audition book. It's an attempt to get right inside the whole process of auditioning, and right inside the heads of both those who perform in auditions and those who judge them. In my many discussions with casting directors, MDs, producers and agents, it seems that we're all equally fascinated and bewildered by the process at times, and nearly everyone agrees that a book that goes beyond the 'how-to' boundaries could be useful in a lot of ways – especially if it can begin with acknowledging the tough questions.

Along with the ones we've just covered I would include: If auditioning is a 'flawed' process, why is that so? Can we simply say that they make performers so nervous that they can never perform at their best in these situations? Can we ever get to the point where the adrenaline rush of nerves just feels like an extra boost of performance energy? What's really going on in our heads and our bodies when we walk into that audition room, and can we ever get to the point where we feel that we can be in control of those mind/body processes? What can we do to give ourselves the best possible chance of showing a panel what we're really capable of? Can we ever get to the point where we feel that we can truly master the process of auditioning?

Every performer I know would like to be able to answer these questions, but I don't know anyone who's ever thought they could. This book sets out to help you create a strategy for really conquering audition challenges – from preparation to performance. And while performance will always remain in the realm of art and not science (meaning that there are no absolute answers to what works and what doesn't), I do believe that there are many things we can learn to control in what is, no doubt, a very unstable process.

We'll start by examining some of the 'neuro' processes that affect us while we're auditioning, and we'll try to understand how and why it is that our emotions often go haywire in audition rooms. We'll be looking closely at the role nerves play in the whole process and how our brains work in these high-stress situations. We'll look at the role that plain hard work, dedication and routine has in our overall confidence and in increasing stamina, and we'll consider how to be more flexible in our learning approaches to material: how to put some elements of risk into our work and how to have the courage to take these riskier choices into auditions. We'll look at how mental preparation affects every element of the process and we'll be considering what really motivates us and how we can better harness that motivation in an attempt to create a kind of audition 'game plan'. In looking at all this our aim is to get to the point where we might begin to understand that elusive 'it' factor and, in a very practical way, get some of it into our own auditions.

We'll finish our journey with a Toolkit that can help us rethink the whole process – from where we've been to where we're headed – and we'll finally understand what it takes to be able to say to ourselves honestly that we're ready to do an audition.

This book is aimed at people who audition in almost any situation. I've spent many years auditioning actors for musical theatre as well as pop singers for both education and the industry. For me the issues covered here are largely applicable to all these areas. Whenever possible I've tried to refer to 'performers' to cover all areas but inevitably some of the exercises are geared more toward acting, simply because whatever you're focusing on – whether it's West End musicals, reality television, film, television or drama school – so much comes down to your relationship with the text that you're trying to communicate. Additionally, this book is based on the premise that knowledge is (a little) power and that the mystery of what makes a great audition is often as prevalent behind a casting desk as it is in front of it.

My hope is that this book can build a little bridge over that desk and enable some much needed 'dialogue' between the person casting and the person auditioning. Auditions are horrible. They're nerve-wracking, panic-inducing and wholly unpleasant. But they're still the only game in town and, having found myself on both sides of the desk many times, I can't help thinking that perhaps with a little more knowledge our auditioning experiences might be a little less fraught.

2 WHAT CAN WE KNOW?

The bleeding obvious

> **Basil:** Can't we get you on *Mastermind*, Sybil? Next
> contestant Sybil Fawlty from Torquay, special subject: the
> bleeding obvious.
>
> *Fawlty Towers*

There must be a reason why so many books on how to audition spend quite so much time on things that should be obvious to anyone with even a modicum of experience and a mildly professional attitude. Surely that reason can only be that no matter how many times we hear it, we still seem to need to be reminded to:

- Be on time
- Be prepared
- Dress appropriately
- Be positive
- Do your research
- Try to be relaxed
- Be yourself
- Treat everyone in the room – whether that's the accompanist or the person who opens the door – with professional courtesy
- Do not allow your nervousness to come across as arrogance
- Don't apologise
- Don't try to be like everyone else – focus on what's unique about you
- Don't make excuses or fumble about
- Don't bring large props or dress up in capes, etc.

Indeed, the list of obvious things is a pretty long one. Yet even the best of the audition advice books seem to feel the need to cover these areas in some detail. That can only be because, as hard as it may be to believe, there are many people who show up to an audition for a part that they *say* they are hoping to get, and yet they still routinely fling down these simple rules and trample upon them.

But is it really the case that many auditionees just can't master these things, which for most auditioning professionals constitute the bleeding obvious?

There just might be two ways to answer that question. One is that we *could* master these things if we just concentrate more, make more effort, pull ourselves together, grow up, etc. The other is that the continual violation of these things just might *mean* something: that we don't really want what we say we want. Or it might mean that we want what we want so badly that we don't know how to handle things when the possibility gets too close, or when the stakes get this high. Don't worry, I'm not about to launch a 'depth psychology' investigation into the spooky inner workings of self-sabotage, but I am willing to bet that all of us know people that we suspect of sabotaging their own success. These people are often a source of mystery – and perhaps some of these people are out there auditioning. But we might take this further and ask what it is that we're talking about when we refer to self-sabotage? On the simplest, armchair-psychology level, we might just conclude that some people are afraid of success.

This is a pretty popular idea – it's one that you encounter quite often when you watch sporting events. Just spend some time watching the final sets at Wimbledon, or the last few holes of the British Open, when the person about to win suddenly seems to go all wobbly. Sports commentators routinely talk about how the player must 'steady the ship' or 'stay focused' – but how do we interpret these comments? Do we assume that the player with the wobbles is sabotaging their own performance, and risking loss? Might that be because they're afraid to win? Is the idea of winning so overwhelming that the hapless tennis player or golfer simply can't face it? Is that really what's going on here? What else would explain their sudden awkwardness and frustrating refusal to 'steady the ship' or to 'stay focused'? Well, I would suggest that there are quite a lot of other things that could be going on here and a word in their ear about pulling themselves together is only likely to prove helpful if the player is in a rational enough state to control their behaviour.

Surely we have to stop a moment here and admit that when we audition we're operating under conditions of extreme pressure. Like the tennis player or the golfer who falls apart at the big moment, our brains simply aren't operating in the usual rational mode. For this reason, we need to look at audition advice and tips a bit differently, because under extreme pressure or moments of heightened emotion the brain just doesn't work in quite the way it does when we're out doing the shopping or dining with friends. At these more relaxed moments we can generally identify a kind of pattern to the ways in which we make decisions about the things we do – even if many of those decisions are not consciously made. But at moments of pressure or heightened emotion we can sometimes feel more confused about our decisions (and their relationship to rationality), and even more confused about the *source* of our decision-making.

Weird science

It may seem a bit of a detour to talk about contemporary studies of the brain, but I promise you it is not. How we react to stress, what we can know about ourselves, and how we judge our own abilities are critical questions for the auditioning performer but the scientific approach to them hasn't really been covered in audition books before. So before we do anything else here, we need to consider just what is going on in our heads when we're under pressure. Consider the pressure of the audition scenario. We're suddenly close to the role or place that we know we're right for, yet we know may be denied to us. We're only a performance away from that siren-song of success and we're in a state where the calm, rational, decision-making part of our mind finds itself swamped by a strange chemical soup that's actually coming from a very different part of our brain than the part that operates when we're going about our usual daily business. We're in the grip of what cognitive scientists might call anticipatory/expectancy-driven emotion. It's a very strange, sometimes irrational place indeed.

Recent studies in the way that fear interacts with anticipatory/expectancy-driven feelings illustrate just how strange we become in this state. Gregory Berns recounts an experiment in which volunteers were given a fairly painful electric shock:

> Every trial began with a statement of how big a shock they were going to receive and how long they had to wait for it, which ranged from one second to almost thirty seconds. For many people, the waiting was worse than the shock. How bad was it? Given a choice, almost every individual preferred to expedite the shock and not wait for it. Nearly a third of the people feared waiting so much that when given the chance, they preferred to receive a bigger shock sooner rather than waiting for a smaller shock later.[1]

Surely this is an extraordinary outcome. Although these participants feared the pain, one third of them feared the anticipation of the pain even more, so in order to avoid the anticipation of a painful shock, they opted for an even more painful one. Proof, surely, that under stressful conditions we make some strange choices.

But why should this be? What is it about stress/fear that makes us do strange things and make irrational decisions? The whole anatomical story of how fear works in the mind and the body is extremely complex and more than we want to go into here. But when we're in fear/stress conditions, the body responds in very specific ways. The 'fear centre' of the brain (the amygdala) springs into action and triggers a cascade of physical events which result in a number of things, such as raised blood pressure, sweaty palms, a racing heart, a dry mouth and a leaden stomach. These physiological reactions are usually present for most auditioning performers and it is a very rare performer indeed who exhibits/experiences no symptoms of the brain's 'fear response' in audition.

Once we're in the grip of this, the 'fear hormones' (which have now spread out, creating all the physiological responses) travel back to the brain, where they can interfere with our cognitive functions. And while we're splashing around in the chemical soup of our temporarily swamped brain, trying to tell ourselves to 'calm down' and 'be cool', the way our brains are wired up is actually *working against us*:

> Interestingly, it is well known that the connections from the cortical areas [the part of the brain where we do our thinking] to the amygdala [the part that triggers fear response] are far weaker than the connections from the amygdala to the cortex. This may explain why it is so easy for emotional information to invade our conscious thoughts, but so hard for us to gain conscious control over our emotions.[2]

All this must begin to dislodge a little of our certainty that good advice can help us make better decisions about our audition behaviour and approach. We might *want* to be positive. We may *try* to relax. But under stressful conditions we can't really be certain that we'll manage either. It may, in fact, be better for us altogether if we just leave our minds alone (an idea we'll consider more closely later).

Clearly, then, it could be the case that this part of our list above (relax, be positive) is beyond simple advice, but what about the other parts? There are surely people who know the obvious, yet still somehow find themselves violating these simple rules. What are we to make of that? The idea behind the audition advice books is a pretty straightforward one: the advice in this book, which you've just read, will lead you to alter your behaviour in a way that helps you to succeed. On the face of it, there's nothing wrong with this idea. Indeed, this idea has fuelled an entire self-help industry. But in truth, this idea proceeds on a big assumption, and we might as well be clear about this from the start.

First, we have to assume that we are all pretty good at *judging* our own behaviour. Then we have to assume that, having judged our own behaviour, we are capable of *altering* it in a way that reflects our acceptance of the good advice. But my experience in the audition room has taught me that between the effects of fear and the anticipatory/expectancy-driven mind-swamp, people are seldom able to judge their own behaviour. And even when given advice, they are often completely incapable of altering the behaviour (as they weren't really aware of how they were behaving in the first place). So it might just be that reading about the bleeding obvious doesn't help quite as much as we might imagine. We must respect the bleeding obvious – of course we must, no self-respecting author who writes audition advice would begin by advising people to ignore these simple things – but perhaps we need to see it differently.

In two minds?

Perhaps it's time to stop shaking our heads in disapproval over the arrogant, the unpleasant, the unprepared, the 'un-self-aware', the apologetic, and try to look a bit deeper to see what's going on here.

Of course it's important to find really sound, helpful people who will not only go over the bleeding obvious but also give you some great overall advice and inside info about cracking into the business.[3] But my point is that good advice isn't the whole story. Even a quick consideration of the list of the bleeding obvious seems to indicate that good advice (and let's face it, every point on the list constitutes good advice) isn't really enough when it comes to the maddening business of auditions. Because good advice – as we generally encounter it – just doesn't take in the whole picture. The whole picture is a strange combination of individual preference, raging neurotransmitters, mysteries of the unconscious and myriad contingencies. Just because these things are difficult to talk about and downright unpredictable (and even more difficult to offer advice on), the only sensible approach for the writer of books on how-to-audition is to take these contingencies as a given of the condition of auditioning. Contingency (in the form of unpredictable personalities, unlucky conditions, uncontrollable nerves, unknowable demands, etc.) is simply a stubborn property of the audition experience, and our best defence against this contingency, or things-we-cannot-control, is to plan for the things we *can* control. I've come to think there are some surprisingly helpful ideas that might just get us past the obvious and into territory that could take the auditioning actor into a slightly finer place amidst those acknowledged contingencies.

Some things on our list above are simple enough: be on time and don't wear a cape are things in most people's control. But some things on our list are quite a bit more troublesome. For starters, let's just consider point number seven on the list: *be yourself.*

It may just have slipped your attention while you've been busy training, rehearsing, auditioning and performing eight shows a week, but in the last forty years or so there's been a kind of revolution going on in research into how the brain operates, called by many (not surprisingly) 'the cognitive revolution'. While this 'revolution' may not seem immediately applicable to the auditioning performer, I promise you that this research has made the ways in which we behave under extreme pressure situations – like auditioning – much clearer. Its advances have reshaped a lot of questions that have long preoccupied philosophers and psychologists. Many of them have to do with things such as how it is that we have a sense of ourselves *as a self,* and how much of our minds we actually have access to. I think George Lakoff and Mark Johnson describe the innovations of the cognitive revolution well:

> Cognitive science is the scientific discipline that studies conceptual systems. It is a relatively new discipline, having been founded in the 1970s. Yet in a short time it has made startling discoveries. It has discovered, first of all, that most of our thought is unconscious, not in the Freudian sense of being repressed, but in the sense that it operates beneath the level of cognitive awareness, inaccessible to consciousness and operating too quickly to be focused on.[4]

They go on to explain that the rule of thumb among the cognitive scientists' fraternity is that a whopping 95 per cent of *all* our thought is unconscious thought. That seems a very surprising percentage to me, and probably does to you as well. But this is backed up by over forty years of research using the powerful new weapons in the neuroscience arsenal. The vastly improved ability to measure brain activity through things like fMRI (functional magnetic resonance imaging) or PET (positron emission tomography) scans have exposed whole areas of brain activity that, up until now, remained largely the preserve of the philosopher and the psychologist. These discoveries are already changing the research landscape – and the non-fiction bestseller lists – in dramatic ways. However, for our purposes I'm interested in focusing on what some of this new research tells us about the limits of self-knowledge, and what those limits mean when we decide that when we walk into that audition room, by god, we're going to be ourselves, and we're going to be brilliant.

The fact is that we all tend to have a kind of 'master narrative' of our lives and of who we are. That narrative serves as the kind of 'authorised' biography of ourselves and often gives us the illusion that we know ourselves and our likes, dislikes, behaviours and thoughts pretty well. But when it comes to the specifics and, rather disturbingly, when it comes to the *important* specifics, we're often a lot less clear about ourselves and our desires. Simple questions that we put to ourselves like: 'Am I sure about what I really want in life?' or 'Am I sure I really love him/her?' are enough to demonstrate how quickly many of us crumble at the moment when we really need to know ourselves. These are just simple examples of conscious uncertainties, but on a very deep level there is much going on in our unconscious thought that can be fairly unsettling when we consider it closely.

For example, it's been demonstrated time and again in numerous studies that other people are more likely to predict our behaviour correctly than we are ourselves. The same goes for having a sense of who we are: according to much scientific study, other people describe us more accurately than we do ourselves, if we take a large average opinion to be right. For example, a study was done in which a group of university students were asked to predict two things: (1) how likely they were to donate money to a charity; and (2) how likely their fellow students were to donate money to a charity. Eighty-three per cent of the students predicted that they themselves would donate. They further predicted that only 56 per cent of the other students would donate. In the end, only 43 per cent of all the students donated. This means that we're more accurate when we're predicting the behaviour of others than when we're predicting our own behaviour, since the students were way off the estimate when it came to predicting for their own behaviour, but not that far off when it came to predicting behaviour for the group overall.[5]

Other, perhaps equally disturbing, research findings have consistently shown that we are:

- Quite likely to abandon principles under pressure or to align our thoughts with others even when they go against our own well worked-out conclusions
- Likely to value ourselves well above average
- Likely to misattribute blame in ways that prevent us from learning by our experiences
- Likely to 'confabulate' when we're not sure about our motives
- Likely to stick to first impressions even when we discover that they're wrong[6]

There's a whole host of other equally strange things that our brains do, not all of them the kind of thing we're likely to approve of and, as Cordelia Fine suggests, if the brain were a person we probably wouldn't invite it to a party.[7] Some of these findings probably surprise us more than others, but all of them undermine any certainty or security we may have when it comes to knowing ourselves or knowing our strengths when we're in front of an audition panel.

As we've seen, predicting our own behaviour is clearly a challenge for us. That's worrying enough when we're thinking about how to approach auditioning and come away with positive results. But even more worrying is what the research has to say about our ability to assess our own skill. There is a fascinating body of research on how we assess ourselves that has been influenced largely by the work of Justin Kruger and David Dunning, the results of which were published in an influential 1999 article called 'Unskilled and Unaware of It: How Difficulties in Recognizing One's Own Incompetence Lead to Inflated Self-Assessments'. The title doesn't leave much to the imagination, and the first part could serve as a theme song for so many auditions I've watched. The research demonstrated two interesting things. The first is that unskilled people will almost invariably overrate their skills significantly when asked to predict how they performed. These people weren't just a little off, they were massively off. For example, a test group who were tested in three areas – grammar, logical reasoning and humour – were asked to predict what their scores would be. The students whose results placed them in the bottom 25 per cent responded by saying that they were confident they would perform at the 60 per cent level or higher. They aren't alone in the overestimation of one's own skill. Further studies have borne out the tendency that human beings have to overestimate their own abilities. In one study of a group of engineers, 42 per cent placed themselves in the top 5 per cent of the group. In another, 97 per cent of academics thought they were performing at a higher than 50 per cent rate. The researchers pointed out that both conclusions are mathematically impossible.[8]

The second interesting thing that came up in the research is that people who fall into the very highest level of skill on testing consistently *underrate* their performance. I think both of these test results are fascinating to contemplate in the realm of auditioning.

First, in the case of the 'unskilled and unaware of it' folk, these findings help make clear why good advice about auditioning is limited in its applicability. If people who rank in the *bottom* 25 per cent of all performers consistently think that they are in the *top* 40 per cent, this goes a long way toward explaining why we see so many poor auditions. The hard fact is that the less skilled people are, the less competence they have in judging their own ability to perform. Therein lies the irony of it: in order to know that they are performing badly, the performers would have to have sufficient expertise in the area of performing to know that they are performing badly. But once they develop sufficient expertise in whatever area they are studying they often do, of course, improve their performances. Consequently, the worst of us can only know how bad we are when we get better. Reading things like this make me wish I'd made the most of those Lloyd Webber auditions by sampling the auditionees. I would be willing to bet that if we asked them before or after they came into the room, the bottom 25 per cent performers would also rate themselves at the 50 or 60 per cent level. This would then explain their heartfelt surprise when they are not advanced to the next round.

Of course, the other side of the question is interesting too: the findings that people in the upper percentile areas consistently mark themselves lower. This doesn't seem hard to understand, as it is surely is just the effect of having attained enough expertise in an area to know how complex and demanding good performance is. Although the Kruger and Dunning studies show that there is an element of comparison with others that significantly affects the ability to assess oneself, 'simply put, these participants assumed that because they performed so well, their peers must have performed well likewise. This would have led [top performers] to underestimate their comparative abilities.'[9]

I feel like that explanation has real resonance with my own experience of auditioning or interviewing. I often think that if I'm able to do what it is that I'm doing, others must be able to do it as well – and possibly do it better – so perhaps I'm not as advanced, skilled, knowledgeable or desirable as I thought, or as they are. It is often, too, the case that advanced performers have a tough balancing act to achieve: on the one hand we need the grit of dissatisfaction with our work to spur us on to harder work and greater performance and on the other, we need to know the difference between excellence and perfection so that we don't consistently undervalue ourselves.

Researcher Dan Ariely has spent much time designing experiments in which he examines the ways in which we come to overvalue our own work. Unlike Kruger and Dunning, he doesn't look specifically at the ratio between skill and overvaluing that skill, but simply at the ways in which we overvalue anything that we've put time into creating. Ariely and his team designed an experiment with some rather complex origami figures: a bird and a frog. On one side he had a group of professional origami artists create the figures, and on the other he had student volunteer 'creators' attempt the same work based on fairly complicated instructions. He then asked for two separate assessments of the completed work. The first group to assess were the volunteer creators themselves, and the second group were simply volunteers who were not involved in the creating of any of the origami birds and frogs. The results clearly demonstrated that being involved in the creation of a work seriously impairs our ability to judge that work:

[The] results showed us that the creators had a substantial bias when evaluating their own work. Noncreators viewed the amateurish art as useless and the professional versions as much, much more exciting. In contrast, the creators saw their own work as almost as good as the experts' origami. It seemed that the difference between creators and noncreators was not in how they viewed the art of origami in general but in the way that the creators came to love and overvalue their own creations.[10]

These findings should probably unsettle us in a number of ways (as well as help to explain all those 'I can't believe they didn't cast me' conversations), and it throws a serious challenge at us in terms of ever being able to view our own work with any level of accuracy.

Because Timothy Wilson works in a different area of research, his book asks the kind of questions that flood into my mind when watching the first few weeks of *American Idol*:

Why don't people realize, eventually, that their conscious conceptions are at odds with their nonconscious personalities? Doesn't it seem that over time people would discover that they are not the person they thought themselves to be? Why didn't Henry Higgins eventually realize that he was not the refined, kindhearted gentleman who abhorred profanity? How can people be so out of touch?[11]

Herding ourselves into a corner

So what does all this have to do with auditions? Well, simply this: when we get advice about just being ourselves in auditions and knowing our strengths, we have to recognise that not only are we probably *not* ourselves in audition (as our brains are most likely too swamped with fear-induced chemicals) we are also *not* the best judge of our skills. Nor are we the most reliable in our ability to predict how we do or will behave. This means that some of the advice we get from books or classes is a bit naïve from the point of view of the way our minds actually work. Might this go some way toward helping us to understand a bit about what is behind those dreadful auditions, where people are clearly not capable of judging themselves? Perhaps. But despite the fact that we are full of surprising mental processes that we don't really control, we still tend to use our own 'master narrative' of ourselves to direct our choices. That is to say that we direct ourselves in given ways, based on past behaviour. The scientist Dan Ariely uses the term 'self-herding' to describe the way in which we herd ourselves in the general direction we think we should go, based on past experience: 'We look at our past actions to inform ourselves of who we are more generally, and then we act in compatible ways.'[12] We'll come back to this idea later, because if Ariely is right we really need to think about how we interpret past actions (out-of-control nerves, audition disasters of one sort or another, numerous rejections and many tearful moments of doubting ourselves) when we're walking through that door into the audition room.

It seems clear that simple advice about 'being yourself' or 'playing to your strengths' is only going to be effective if you have a pretty accurate idea of *who you are*: what your strengths are, what you're good at and what's unique about you. It sounds straightforward enough, but years of auditioning have taught me that having the answer to any of these questions is quite a tall order. You might also suppose that spending a few years in training should be enough to help people realise where their strengths lie (as throughout most training programmes, students are continually hearing feedback about their performances, particularly in terms of what's working and what isn't), and to help them know themselves and their strengths as performers. But my experience is that the will to delude ourselves, or perhaps to keep reinventing ourselves or simply to cling stubbornly on to our own convictions, is a strong one.

Clearly, it's tough for us to figure out who we are and why we're doing things – either by ourselves or even with some help – and it can be even tougher to give ourselves direction. Specifically, directions like 'try to relax' or 'don't be scared'. But if it's hard for the auditioning performer to know their own mind, casting directors can have just as much difficulty in knowing why and how they respond to the people that walk into the room. We know, for example, that there are many situations in our own lives where we make some pretty snap decisions about people that we don't know all that well. It is in fact very common to have strong reactions to people for reasons that we can't explain. Sometimes we can actually point to something – a sound, a look, a manner – that we find irritating, but not always. I have a good friend who launches into an absolute tirade if the subject of a certain television presenter comes up. He will go on passionately about just how horrible this particular presenter is, but of course he never really manages to get to grips with just why he gets so irritated. Words like 'smug', 'annoying', 'bland', or 'insipid' inevitably make an appearance in the conversation, but never does he get into the detail of why this particular (and very popular I might add) presenter is smug, annoying or bland. In other words: what makes him so? Well, I will probably never find out because I doubt if he really knows himself.

But just as we often have irrational dislikes of someone we barely know, we can often have irrationally positive responses too. It isn't that we don't entirely have a clue in all cases: often we do or don't like someone instantly just because they remind us strongly of someone we know. But it is also true that we pick up cues from the look and the sound of people that influence our judgement without ever involving the rational, decision-making part of the brain.

For example, the sound of a voice can lead us into some quick judgements. Logically, we know that the sound of someone's voice isn't a reliable measure of their heart or their head or their personality. Nevertheless, research shows that we make these snap judgements anyway:

The results provide[d] clear evidence that listeners use ... acoustic properties in making personal attributions to speakers. Speakers with high-pitched voices were judged less truthful, less emphatic, less 'potent' (smaller, thinner, faster), and more nervous. Slow-talking speakers were judged less truthful, less fluent, and less persuasive and were seen as more 'passive' (slower, colder, passive, weaker) but more 'potent'.[13]

We know, too, that we have similar responses to faces, but don't know exactly why. This response turns out to be more context-dependent. In other words, we rate certain kinds of faces differently in specific situations. In his book, *Flipnosis*, Kevin Dutton describes the ways in which people who either have 'baby faces', or those faces that grow into a more mature look, fare differently in different contexts:

> Researchers have, in fact, uncovered all sorts of differences between baby-faced and mature-faced individuals. Or, more specifically, in the ways we interact with them. In relationships, women are more likely to confide in a baby-faced friend than in one who looks more mature. In the courtroom, baby-faced defendants are more likely to be found guilty of crimes involving negligence than those involving intentional misconduct. And in the workplace, baby-faced individuals are less likely to hold positions of power.[14]

But these pretty general appraisals of people's faces seem obvious. Some are more difficult to pin down because some responses depend on the actual 'chemistry' of the perceiving person:

> In a jaw-mashing blow to Arnold Schwarzenegger and his pals, [it's been] found that women, on average, actually prefer men's faces when they are made just that little bit more like their own. When they are *feminised*, in other words ... But during ovulation the trend mysteriously reverses. For women who are ovulating, it's actually *masculine* facial features that prove the bigger turn-on.[15]

So, our faces, our voices, our similarities to people that audition panel members might have loved or hated, and whether there are ovulating or non-ovulating female panellists: all these things can be part of a snap judgement of us as we walk into that room – and this is before we even finish our first monologue or dance or song. No doubt all of these things feed into the elusive 'it' that we may or may not come across as having. And of course, this part of their response to your work is largely beyond your control.

Summary

So what can we learn from our initial brief romp through contemporary research on brain and behaviour? Surely at the very least we must recognise that there is a *lot* of irrational behaviour and judgement going on in audition rooms all over the world. I've sat on many panels and been awed by the strength of response to people's auditions that I can only describe as, if not irrational, certainly out of proportion to the performance that I just saw. I've seen incredibly inept people swear that performing is the only thing they can ever imagine doing with their lives. I've seen extremely talented people give up on themselves. I've seen bland performers swear that they're fascinating, and tenors who say they're baritones. I once watched an older panel member swear to the rest of us that a *very* untalented young lady (who we were all amazed had made it this far) was going to be the 'next big thing'.

So do we all just lose our ability to be rational when it comes to the whole process of auditioning? Should we give up the whole idea of trying to decide for ourselves whether we're any good or not, since we clearly aren't good judges of ourselves? Is it time to give up trying to 'be ourselves' or trying to tell ourselves to 'just relax' once our fear responses have kicked in? Are we simply at the mercy of crazy audition-panel responses or perhaps the reaction our 'baby faces' might inspire in them? Well, probably not. The fact is, we may be limited in our effectiveness in some ways, but once we can understand the nature of those limitations, I believe we'll be better able to equip ourselves to work within them.

The point in looking at all this is simply to acknowledge all the ways in which the audition process is complicated. I've always been aware that when I'm asked to give advice in audition workshops (which, of course, I am expected to do), most of the questions that come up remind me of the fact that to really explain just how complicated the process is would take a long time. Although I don't expect that simply understanding these things will immediately increase anyone's chances of audition success, I *do* think that before we attempt to make a living at a business that relies on auditions in order to get a job, we should, from the outset, be clear about the fact that there are many things involved in the process – and that not all of them are related simply to talent or even to rational thinking. I believe that once we acknowledge those complications we will be better prepared to take them on.

I think what all the science demonstrates is that when we talk about someone having that 'it' factor, there are really good reasons why we can't articulate what 'it' is. We can't be articulate about this because some of the things that make up the 'it' factor are connected with some of the irrational ways in which we both behave and perceive things in auditions. But even if it's hard to articulate I feel pretty certain that, after many years of watching auditions, there are three tangible things present when a performer really astonishes or impresses an audition panel (or perhaps has that 'it' factor). Crucially, they are all things in our control:

- Mastery (which requires stamina)
- Risk-taking (which requires courage and flexibility)
- Confidence (which comes from having the two qualities above)

Maybe we can't do much about our baby face, or the occasional knee-jerk response from a panel member, but we *can* do something about all three of these critical elements. This brief investigation into all the irrationalities of auditioning should hopefully inspire an important conclusion: we have to concentrate on and conquer the things in our control, because there are so many things in the audition process that we have no control over. That means that we need a serious strategy and a carefully worked-out plan in order to get to a point where we're ready to take on the challenge of auditioning.

But before we start, we need a better understanding of all the things that are affecting us when we perform under pressure. We can't plan and embrace a strategy for defeating our fear unless we know a lot more about how it works. In the next two chapters we'll be looking very specifically at the role that fear plays in these situations, both in terms of how it affects our brain function, and in terms of how its powerful ability to suppress risk can interfere not only with our performance but also with the kinds of choices we make in preparation and interpretation.

3 METAPHORICAL WEIGHT GAIN AND OTHER SIDE-EFFECTS OF AUDITIONING

The not so bleeding obvious

. . . there was a particular audition; it was a final call for *Les Misérables* back in 2002. It started out fine but midway through the prepared material my heart began to beat harder than normal and I began to feel light headed, to the point where I thought I may pass out! I was shocked as it came on so suddenly. In the end the 'episode' affected the 'money notes' and the panel were clearly disappointed that I had messed up. As I was walking out I started to sweat profusely and it culminated in me bursting into tears on the street in frustration! I had spent weeks working on the material and felt ready and prepared. It affected my confidence for a little while . . .

One thing most people agree on is that auditions are scary. I've spent much time in audition rooms trying to ease the nerves of those auditioning. Fear (as the actor above so neatly illustrates) can cause some extraordinary responses in our bodies, most of which we recognise, although we may not comprehend just how and why our bodies react so strongly to fear, or even why a relatively simple thing like auditioning can invoke such terror. Okay, we're being judged, and we may really want this part, but should it cause such profound effects that it sometimes renders us completely incapable of doing what we came to do? Well, this is not an easy question to answer and the answers we do find are not as straightforward as we might think on first consideration.

Perhaps the critical question is: How does fear work in audition situations? Audition fears are largely 'learned' fears. For many of us, the memory of our first audition (if we can remember it) usually involves fear. But because we've never experienced an audition before, we can't – in this 'audition-virgin' state – be expressing a *learned* fear reaction to auditions themselves. We can, however, be expressing a learned fear reaction that is associated with things like fear of rejection or fear of the unknown. We may have experienced similar situations such as job interviews, tests, or performing under scrutiny that also helped to kick in a learned fear-response. In a very informal survey of actor pals, it seems that the reasons behind the fear of auditioning are pretty numerous: from the more obvious fear of rejection, to the fear of getting our hopes up too high or the fear of being in a room with powerful people. But let's consider that 'audition-virgin' state. At this point what we may have been frightened of is simply the unknown. But it could also be that we were simply afraid of doing in public what we had only done in private up until now. Or it may be that we were seeing the audition as something akin to a final examination. Just how powerful our fear responses were would depend on the kinds of experiences we had had with the unknown, or performing in public, or final examinations. However we approach it, we know that it would be a rare person indeed who felt no fear at their first audition. The extent of their fear would almost certainly depend on their previous experiences in these realms. This is because, as neuroscientist Antonio Damasio points out, the brain has the ability to amplify or decrease further emotional reactions to any given stimulus, or 'fear trigger'. We're in some fairly complicated territory here, but it's worth considering since so much of what drives audition experience in terms of perception, behaviour and emotion is connected to the way in which we respond to the 'fear trigger'.

How fear works

In order to help us create some strategies for conquering (or at least coping with) our fear, we need to take a little detour here and learn about what's going on when we have responses as strong as the one described by the actor at the start of this chapter. Antonio Damasio

– one of the world's foremost researchers into the connection between brain and body – considers the ways in which emotion is triggered and then leads to some response, and describes two pathways in which a single stimulus can create a state of emotion. He recognises that there is an element of memory that, along with the initial fear response, can determine whether that emotion is heightened or lessened. The process he describes between stimulus (walking into audition room) and emotion (fear) can 'spread laterally into parallel chains of events' and create a kind of cascade effect. 'As time unfolds . . . additional stimuli may sustain the triggering of the same emotion, trigger modifications of it, or even induce conflicting emotions.'[1] In other words, our brains have time to assemble all the memories associated with, or triggered by, this particular scary situation. These additional memories may be either good or bad. Perhaps the memories may be that we've been successful in this situation before (hence some *abatement* of our fear). Or perhaps we remember that it's all gone disastrously wrong in this situation before (hence the *amplification* of fear). While all this is going on, of course, we still have to make some decisions about our actions in the audition room. According to Damasio, there are two ways in which we can make these decisions about our actions when we're in a fear-inducing situation.

The first is through reason (Path A) and the second is through quick, gut reaction (Path B). However, as we've seen before when in an audition our brain isn't in its usual everyday state, and our access to reasoned decision-making is limited by what our audition experiences in the past have been (and how those memories, if scary, amplify our fear). If we're lucky, our fear response might be lessened through experience (and most actors say that they get less afraid as they gain experience) or abated perhaps by past successes (which could happen through any number of other things, such as recognising someone on the panel who has been encouraging to you before, or being treated with kindness and respect). If our fear response has been lessened, then it's likely that we'll be in a position employ Path A and we'll be able to reason out our actions before we act. But if our fear response has been amplified by remembering some painful experiences associated with walking into an audition room, we will almost certainly employ Path B. The interesting thing about Path B is that in cases of real fear it seems that we bypass the reasoning, thinking (cortical), areas of the brain altogether, which means, effectively, that we are putting fear in the driver's seat. And that, no doubt, must be the mental equivalent of Mr Toad's wild ride in *The Wind in the Willows*!

If we think a little harder about this it doesn't seem surprising. Our fear response has evolved as an important part of our survival. When we're seriously threatened the stimuli goes straight to a small, almond shaped bit of the brain buried deep in the centre, called the amygdala, which sends instructions to the body before the higher reasoning areas of the brain are involved. Joseph LeDoux, who has devoted his life to the study of fear and fear response, explains that some stimuli go right to the amygdala, and cause bodily responses before we can think about them. This is a kind of evolutionary wisdom because, as he points out, if we get distracted by a decision-making process while facing up to a sabre-toothed tiger we would probably be eaten before we could decide what to do next. Consequently, the body responds before the brain can interfere, and that might just be the thing that keeps us alive in tough, threatening situations.[2]

If you've ever wondered why your body goes a bit haywire before an audition you really don't have to look much further than this as an explanation. Auditions invoke anything from mild fear to absolute terror and the body responds quickly under that threat, as we considered earlier. In fact, a quick assessment of your physical symptoms will give you an excellent picture of just how high your fear level is in audition situations. You may find yourself with an altered breathing pattern, racing heart, sweaty palms, dry throat, etc. There's an interesting addition to these physical 'fear response' feelings that Damasio calls a 'somatic marker'. These are a kind of emotional signal – literally a 'gut feeling' – that manifests itself in the body at key moments. These emotional signals can be quite strong and while Damasio states that an emotional signal is no substitute for clear, rational and considered decision-making, it is still a *part* of that decision-making and can influence the efficiency, speed or even the outcome of a decision. These kinds of gut feelings are precisely the kind that we might experience when we're about to answer the phone, when we're waiting for an audition decision, when we know we're about to hear bad news, or when we're about to open that door and walk into an audition room. Some people describe this as butterflies, and some as a leaden feeling in their stomachs, but much of what we feel at the moment of walking into an audition will be influenced by all our previous experiences of opening a door and walking into an audition room.

We all know the power of emotion, and certainly as actors we're aware of how difficult it can be to self-generate anything with the power of true fear or true anger or true obsession. We have many ways in which we simulate these things – some better than others – but we know very well that we couldn't do our job as actors if we were truly in the throes of genuine fear or anguish or fury. Equally, we know how hopeless we can feel when we try to control emotions that we're already feeling by telling ourselves – as we're about to open that door – to stay calm, stay positive, breathe deeply, etc.

As the experience related at the start of this chapter demonstrates, the power of our own emotions to sabotage, frighten and overwhelm us, or block our access to material that we know well, can be both surprising and uncontrollable. Furthermore, most of this emotional activity seems far from our conscious control. As Damasio explains, emotional signals can sometimes operate 'under the radar of consciousness', and these workings can affect the decisions or actions we take. It's important to keep in mind that in our evolutionary way we are wired to choose the action that is most likely to result in 'the best possible outcome, given prior experience'.[3]

This neatly captures the way in which a lot of our brain activity is unconscious (operating 'under the radar') and it also neatly describes the ways in which fear is related to ensuring our survival and to ensuring the 'best possible outcome' for ourselves. But initially, reading Damasio's description might give us cause to be a bit sceptical: surely when it comes to auditioning, the action most likely to lead to the 'best possible outcome' is for us to perform our faultless, luminous, inspired and utterly brilliant rendition of whatever it was we prepared? If that is the best possible outcome, why is it that, once we walk into that room, our emotional signals don't always lead us to a brilliant performance? Why is it that, instead, they play havoc with our heartbeat, make our palms sweat, make us forget things we know perfectly well and generally turn in a performance that was nothing like as good as our rehearsal?

Well, here's the twist. Your *conscious* idea of the best possible outcome ('I get this fabulous lead role on the West End') might very well not be your *unconscious* brain/body's idea of the best possible outcome in this given moment ('get out of here fast, this kind of experience has humiliated you before').

From this basis we can reason out a number of things. One is that fear is a mechanism that can put us in a confoundedly contradictory state when we're in an audition situation. Consciously we want the part. We came here to get the bloody part! But somewhere in the hippocampal region of our brain memory is simmering away, reaching back into our past and drawing up those excruciating moments of painful rejection, self-perceived humiliation, complete loss of text or some other 'audition disaster', and is redisplaying them for us just as we walk in the door. Now something else has kicked in, triggered by the fear emotion itself: suddenly the memory of past fear comes flooding in, putting us in a double bind. We're at war with ourselves and we probably don't even know it. The part of our brain that we perceive as the 'driver' – the executive brain function – has brought us here to audition and, indeed, it insists that we are going to stay here and see the thing out. But the part of our brain that stores trauma and old feeling may well be telling us to run away as fast as possible.

Now, as we've considered, we may just be 'audition virgins'. Surely in this case there are no specific memories that come flooding back to us as we walk through that door with our CV and headshots in hand? Well, perhaps this is the point where we start to realise all of the things that auditions come to represent to us and why they can trigger fear and memory in some pretty specific ways, whether we've auditioned before or not. Let's imagine that the person going for the audition has never auditioned before. What things could be swimming around in both the conscious and unconscious mind? That is likely to depend on what the audition means (beyond something obvious like a part on *Casualty*), and this depends on just how much metaphorical 'weight' we load onto any given audition. That metaphorical weight could be made up of any or all of the following things:

- I was right to study acting (despite what my parents thought)
- I *am* capable of acting at a professional level
- I am successful
- This job validates my belief in myself (even if I still have self-doubts)
- I can make a living doing what I love (and I can finally quit that job I hate)
- People want me (even if only for this show)
- Whatever else happens, I'll always have this on my CV
- This job opens doors and will lead to more work.

Of course, in a significant way success at any job interview or audition carries all of this need for validation and metaphorical weight with it. We say we're auditioning or we're interviewing, but really we're testing ourselves against the world; against our competition. We're looking for validation and to be reassured that we're on the right path, to know that we're worthy, to know that we're making the right decisions for ourselves and for our careers. So in a very real sense that extra weight means that we're exposing our hearts and our desires in a way that leaves us quite vulnerable. Surely this alone is enough to give us a concrete understanding of why fear is such a big part of the audition process, whether we're 'audition virgins' or not, and helps us understand that while some of the fear we may experience is specific *to* auditions (Will I remember my monologue? Will I hit that note in my break? Will I remember to smile during the interview?), much of it has to do with the ways in which we've 'loaded' the audition in such a way that (if successful) it will validate us and vindicate our life choices. While it's only natural that we pile expectation on any given audition, it is critical to remember that the more metaphorical weight we load onto the audition experience, the stronger will be our experience of the fear factor (and its physical and mental symptoms).

The real scale of this fear means that much of what we do in an audition room may be far more out of our conscious control than we might think. Interestingly, actors who have been auditioning for long periods of time often report that their fear levels fluctuate, sometimes going up but more often going down. This is, no doubt, because over time the prefrontal cortex (the thinking part of the brain) gains experience in putting the amygdala into check during audition situations. We've done them, we've won them, we've lost them, we know that we'll live whatever happens, and we gradually come to be more 'at home' with the audition routine. While this makes good sense and bears out much of the research into the ways that experience helps to quell fear, this process isn't rock solid for everyone. Indeed, for some people the fears grow worse or are triggered by (sometimes unconscious) things that bring on their worst memories of the audition experience (the memory 'cascade') and this is enough to spark up the amygdala and override the prefrontal cortex's attempt to calm things down. Not surprisingly, some actors say that the fear depends on how much they want the job, and many report incidents where they auditioned for things they didn't particularly want and were surprised to be offered them. In these cases they always report that their usual audition nerves were almost entirely quelled as they weren't too keen on the job anyway.

If this anecdotal evidence is at all valid, it surely means that we're most able to take good audition advice (be polite, be positive, be yourself, try to be relaxed, don't make excuses, etc.) when we don't really care about the job. In other words, good advice seems to be most useful for us right at the point when we don't need it. Of course, it may also mean that when we really want the job our fear levels will rise enough to interfere significantly with our ability to do anything the way that we've been advised to, and we simply turn the whole experience over to 'Mr Toad'. In the midst of this wild ride of fear we may somehow seem arrogant when we thought we were being confident, or we may suddenly seem unpleasant when we thought we were being professional. We may find our mind goes blank when just a moment ago it was crammed with the words of our prepared speech, or we may see words swimming around on a page in front of us instead of forming logical, comprehensible sentences. With our minds and bodies temporarily swamped in the chemical soup of fear we suddenly find that we're no longer the best judge of our actions, and no longer the captain of our ship of conscious behaviour.

To me, the obvious things that comes of looking at all this are the ways in which old sayings like 'success breeds success' start to make sense. Of course, if your memories as you walk in the door are of your heart sinking when you hear the news that the contract went to someone else, or of the many rejections you've sustained over years of audition, those memories will come flooding back to amplify your fear response. But if the result of walking through that door had always (or nearly always) been a subsequent phone call in which you are told that the audition went brilliantly and you are going to be offered the part, it's likely that these memories work to *abate* rather than amplify fear, and may just give you a significant advantage over everyone else waiting to go through the door. So the strength of our fear is likely to be contingent on a wide range of factors, including our own natural disposition (some of us are more at home with risk than others), our own audition history and experience, all the ways in which the audition may be metaphorically representing something else in your life (a need for validation or love of some sort, a way of proving the naysayers wrong, a chance to redefine yourself, etc.), or just how appealing this particular part is to you.

Along with acknowledging just how strong and how complex the workings of fear are in audition situations, we need to consider the other kinds of effects fear can have on us. Specifically, we need to consider the way that fear inhibits our ability to make exciting, inspired, unique (and risky) decisions in audition performance.

4 RISKY BUSINESS

Suppose for a moment we could describe the kind of impression we hope to make in an audition. There are probably a lot of answers to this question, but it seems reasonable to assume that we would want to stand out from the competition in a positive way. But how can we do that? Of course, one of the great difficulties about auditioning is that we so rarely get the chance to observe our competition in action. But if it helps, I can tell you from experience what it is that makes the panel's eyes glaze over when watching the one-hundredth audition of the day. It's what I think of as a 'reasonably good' performance. You probably know the thing I mean: it's the kind of audition I described at the beginning of this book. It's an audition that can be described as safe, as 'accomplished'. You can see some evidence of training, some intelligence and clarity, some connection with the material, but no spark. No courage. Nothing that stands out. No risk.

Making a strong impression is always about taking a risk. The general lack of risk is what makes so many audition panels begin to grumble about drama-school graduates. I've always been particularly sensitive to this grumbling when I hear it – and believe me, I hear a lot of it – because, along with the professional audition work I do, I've spent much time in drama schools training students. I've done a bit of grumbling myself about the fact that while panels may not be excited by the 'drama-school grad auditionee', they would be even *less* excited by working with a company full of young people who'd had no training whatsoever. The truth of this observation is always accepted by my casting colleagues when I make the argument, and of course all of them say how much they value training. But I have still watched some of them carry a bit of that anti-drama-school prejudice into the room with them. And after years of auditioning drama-school grads, I find myself beginning to understand their feelings on the subject.

What I worry about with training is that sometimes it knocks the risk out. Of course, it's important to have the basics – where to breathe, how to centre yourself; how to use the voice, all of that, but some places do knock out the character of the person. And that does worry me. On some courses the first year is taken up entirely by stripping that person of all personality and charm. And then the second year they start to build that student up again. And I think that's a bad way to go, because who knows what they're building?

David Grindrod

Overall, panels get put off many drama-school grads by what they think looks 'too polished'. I've also heard 'too considered', 'too careful', 'too much alike' or 'too eager to please'. But hang on (you may be thinking!), isn't that what we think audition panels want: a polished, considered performance and an 'eager to please' personality? It's enough to make any drama-school grad throw up their hands in despair. Is it true that all the training, polish and care can work against you? Well, the sad answer is yes, *if* what it results in looks too coached and too careful. In fact, it is true that a great majority of drama-school grads leave a panel in exactly the position described in the little scenario that opens this book: 'what to do with this one?' They are often the very definition of *competence without the 'it' factor*. They get lost because, at the end of the audition, the only impression that they leave is that they are competent and pleasant: not, you must agree, a *strong* impression, and after days of watching auditions, panels only really respond to strong impressions.

Strong impressions, however, usually involve a little risk. So what kind of risk? And how risky are we talking here? Well, the word gets used a lot and although we certainly understand what it means, I'm not sure any of us really examine closely enough what it means in a performance context. So when a member of an audition panel tells you not to play it safe, to take some risk, what are they really talking about?

When we're talking about risk we're not just talking about behaviour. We're also talking about the ways in which we appraise or assess things before act upon them. Unless we're in the midst of some crisis – facing a hungry lion, balancing on the edge of a precipice, looking down the barrel of a gun, or sometimes, as we've seen above, about to walk into an audition room – we tend to think before we make a decision about our actions.

So, let's take a few steps back from the moment when we walk through the door into the audition room. Let's go back to the point where we're rehearsing and making some initial decisions about how we'll approach and interpret our material. At these moments we're under no particular threat, so we're unlikely to do something spontaneous or to exhibit a true gut-level reaction. Instead, we size up the problem: we make some decisions about what we think will be rational and reasonable choices for a character to be making at a given moment. The question, of course, is what leads us to these choices, and no doubt we have some kind of rational process that we bring to our performance work.

Let's imagine that we have decided to sing 'Send In The Clowns' for an audition and that our entire purpose is to keep Frederick from thinking that we're heartbroken. So every choice we make from there is connected to the desire to make Frederick believe that we're older, wiser, too philosophical and too full of good humour to let the situation tear us apart. But of course, we also know that our heart is utterly, utterly broken. So we have an interesting situation for an actor to play. The audience must know that I'm devastated, but Frederick must not.

A really close listen to Sondheim's song – both the lyrics and the fairly mournful and nocturnal sound of piano – would certainly make this reading logical and valid. Now suppose we watch a skilled performer take this into an audition and one member of the panel concludes that the performance was 'safe'. There was no risk. What are they talking about? Are they talking about the interpretive choices? Perhaps – you could certainly make some riskier interpretive choices. Are they talking about the performance itself? Possibly – we'd have to see the performance. But everything I've just written assumes that you and I really know what 'risk' means and why a member of an auditioning panel would value it so highly, and why taking more of a risk might have made this performance seem to be more vibrant, and why so many directors, actors and acting teachers like to talk about risk as if it is a very positive thing indeed.

Of course, dictionary definitions of risk are not quite so positive in their descriptions. You can find various combinations of words but generally dictionaries define risk as: a hazard; the probability of a return that is less than expected; a source of danger; the possibility of incurring loss; being exposed to loss or damage; gambling against the odds; the likelihood of an unfavourable condition, etc.

Can it really be the case that something with such potentially dangerous outcomes is the thing that we should be aiming for in audition or performance? Is it true that we must expose ourselves to loss in order to make an impression? Do we have to thumb our noses at probability to be successful? Maybe – and we'll look at this later – but is this really what we mean when we talk about risk in performance or audition? I think not. I think we've come to use the word to mean something else.

We're all natural-born appraising animals that assess and calculate risks before taking action. We're hard-wired with risk-averse tendencies and can't help *thinking things through*. I don't think that the director, the casting agent or the acting teacher – when they ask you to take a risk – are asking you to stop thinking, stop assessing, or stop calculating the outcome of things. However, I do think that what they're suggesting is that when it comes to performance, *logic isn't your only tool*. In fact, logic, reason, appraisal, calculation, assessment – whatever you want to call it – if solely relied upon, is likely to take the edge off a performance. Now why is that?

I don't think there's a single straightforward answer here, or one that isn't tautological (i.e., logic is too logical, reasoning is too reasonable or analysing is too analytical). But perhaps the tautology is helpful in this case. What it seems to demonstrate is that the sphere in which our reason works is a reasonable one, and you can imagine just how an audition panel might feel about a logical, reasonable, analytical performance. Ah – I hear you say – but we don't use just logic, we use emotion. Well, that's correct up to a point. You use the emotional skill you have to express the choices you've come onto in an analytical way.

In the case above I've made the analytical choice to make Frederick think that I'm older, wiser and not utterly heartbroken, and the emotion that I might employ in achieving that is an extension (a servant, I might say) of my reasoned decision to affect Frederick in this way. But what if I *didn't* start my analysis with logic in the first place? What if I started from a purely physical/emotional point? What if I started simply with a photograph of an old man that I felt both repulsed by and sympathetic toward? What if I left analysis out of it altogether and just stared at that photograph and let it lead me wherever it might? I might imagine my skin crawling if he touched me. I might imagine how strangely thin his hair would feel if I touched it in sympathy when he looked overwhelmed at the thought of losing his young wife. I might ask myself if my sense of tenderness toward him could overcome any revulsion I might feel at his touch. I might look at him and remember that I've always hated his ears. I might suddenly wonder, as I look at those ears, if I've ever known or understood what love really is. And I might decide that his ears have given me the nearly uncontrollable urge to laugh. Would I come up with a better performance? Who knows? There are no guarantees when you're working without the 'logical' net, but it would almost certainly lead you somewhere *different*. And different is, in itself, is a start.

Perhaps some other examples can help make this clearer. I once directed some young, but particularly fine actors in *Henry IV*. We were doing the scene where Prince Hal slays Hotspur. Both Nathan (Hal) and Carl (Hotspur) had studied stage combat and we were able, collaboratively, to put together a pretty fine scene of exciting stage sword-wizardry. We realised about two weeks into rehearsal that the scene just didn't work. It wasn't that it didn't convince us physically that Hal was killing Hotspur. It just didn't move us as we watched it. It had no spark. We tinkered and analysed and restaged, but whatever we did somehow just didn't have an emotional impact. One day we took a break from rehearsing and in a playful moment the actor playing Falstaff picked up Hotspur's sword. He and Nathan had a very funny moment of drunken sword fighting and suddenly we decided that it might be quite funny if Prince Hal had learned all his sword-fighting skills from Falstaff. We laughed as we watched Falstaff give a very funny drunken sword-fighting lesson to his young companion, explaining the virtues of dodging and running just at the key moments.

As the rest of the company drifted back into the room we resumed rehearsal, but Nathan was still remembering his playful lessons with Falstaff and played his side of the fight as if he were showing how much he had learned about cowardly sword fighting. It was funny and the whole company enjoyed it because once Nathan's swordsmanship became so useless, and somewhat comical, it took away all the precision of Carl's carefully choreographed responses and the fight suddenly had the strange messy look of a real barroom brawl. In the midst of these antics, Nathan made a final, funny 'stage' thrust, which came at entirely the wrong moment of the choreographed fight, and Carl – who had no choice but to admit that his character had been mortally slain by an incompetent swordsman – laughed, as he said 'O, Harry, thou hast robb'd me of my youth!'

Suddenly the rehearsal room went quiet. Hotspur's bitter speech continued but the emphasis slyly switched from bitterness over Prince Hal's superior sword fighting to bitterness and laughter about being slain by a fool. Throughout his speech, Hotspur's bitterness never really lost its combination of shock, irony and humour. As the actor played his death, we realised that our five-minute rehearsal break follies had stumbled across something interesting and strangely moving. We kept it in. Once the show opened, every time that fight took place – every time Carl dropped his sword, looked down at his bloody hand, and laughed before dying – I cried. As we ran it, I got to the point where I would look around and I realised that the unexpected combination of blood and laughter made many people in the audience cry. It's not that the choice was totally illogical – I'm sure I'm not the only one who's wondered on reading *Henry IV* how a barfly like Prince Hal could defeat a master warrior like Hotspur – but suddenly the very ineptness of Hal's swordplay, the way that it played havoc with a superior swordsman's expectation, and the way that Hotspur could not help but find it funny that this drunken fool had got the better of him, made sense.

What is instructive for our purposes is that it didn't come initially from a logical place.

Was it risky? I'd say so – I worried about it all the way up to opening, as you do when you're finding something unusual incredibly moving but can't be sure whether it really is, or if it's just your own strange emotional response. The risk paid off in this case. But it doesn't mean that there weren't times when I thought we should go back to something a bit more 'standard stage choreography sword death'.

A year or so later I was directing *The Hired Man*. At one point in the musical there's a song of farewell as the men go off to fight in the war. It's a slightly dull moment in the piece, probably because it doesn't really advance the story apart from showing us the tearful goodbyes. We moved it around, improvised around it, but simply couldn't find a way (while working with the song) to give the scene any real depth or any sense of how potentially tragic the situation was. One evening during an early run I realised that we were missing one of the 'girlfriends' on stage. I don't remember why we didn't stop, but we didn't. As the song and the goodbyes progressed, the lone actor/soldier began to pace the front of the stage, looking and hoping that his 'girlfriend' would show up before the song finished. But as he did so he suddenly decided to draw on his own imagination and play the scene as a young soldier frightened to the marrow that, while all around him people were hugging and kissing their loved ones, he was about to leave and face his possible death all alone. In the meantime the young actress, who had wandered out of the theatre, heard the music, realised she was late and burst in through the front of house doors. The actor waiting for her screamed her name and she screamed his back. She scrambled up on to the stage, helped by the other women and as he threw his arms around her he burst into tears and so did she. The song was nearing the finish, where the soldiers had to walk up the ramp to their ship and suddenly the company members joined in the improvised moment, dragging the young tearful soldier away from his girlfriend who was, at this point, overcome herself by her lateness and at nearly missing the moment. Of course we kept it in, and when the show ran it became the one moment that reduced the audience to tears and made them realise what was at stake for these young men about to go into battle.

I recount these stories, because I've learned over years of directing that logic isn't my only tool, and that impulse or inspiration or gut feelings don't always solve my artistic riddles either. I've just learned that when I'm stuck it's time to approach a problem obliquely rather than directly. I don't hammer a scene over and over again when we can't get it right – I've learned that it will only lead to more discussion (analysis, rationality, etc.). Instead, at these moments, I find it best to take a break and let everyone's imagination wander or simply play. I've learned never to ignore strange or off-the-wall impulses when I'm working and I try never to worry about how much time I might 'squander' this way because inspiration grows in some pretty strange places.

However, simply telling yourself to take more risk when you audition is like telling yourself to calm down, to be positive, etc. It's good advice – of course it is – but how can you take it on if the hard truth is that human beings are naturally risk averse? There are volumes of research done in this area that are often contradictory in terms of what specific conditions are more or less likely to inspire us to take a risk, but it doesn't take a research grant and lots of poorly paid undergraduate volunteers to figure out that, in general, it is in our interest to be wary about taking risks. Clearly there are times when we're even less willing than usual to do so, and one of these times is when we're seeking approval – or a lead role in *Les Mis*.

So how can we know when a risk will pay off? Well, we can't. That's why it's a risk. But surely in a situation that's already fraught with danger – like an audition – we would be foolish to add more danger by doing something risky? Yes. That is absolutely true, and it's an important thing to remember. In fact, you might want to hang this sign on your wall:

> **Auditions are risky enough.
> So don't add to your danger
> by doing something risky.**

Of course, underneath it, you'll also have to hang this sign:

> **The riskiest thing you can do in an
> audition . . . is to play it safe.**

It's an irritating conundrum, and if we can't respond to our own direction to 'take risks' (any more than we can respond to our own direction when we tell ourselves to 'just forget it' or 'try to be confident' or 'calm down') then we have only one choice here: We have to learn to create the conditions in which things like risk-taking can come about (time, patience, curiosity, openness and willingness to work outside our logical safety zone). We have to learn to create the conditions in which the confidence to take risks comes about (absolute belief in our own expertise and mastery). It also means that we have to learn to create the conditions in which we have some ability to handle our fear (by perfecting our 'mental game').

The plain fact is that fear inhibits us and makes us risk averse. If you think about it, that is its whole purpose: the last thing we need, when facing danger, is the urge to play in an uninhibited way or to suddenly pull out the unexpected. If we're truly fearful we just *can't* take risks. Fear works like a drug that takes the edge off our wilder impulses. Like any effective drug, of course, there are side-effects, and those side-effects are related to the dosage. A very large dose of fear – staring down the barrel of a loaded gun, being attacked by a lion – has incredible side-effects that include full-blown shock (with symptoms running from increased heartbeat to oxygen deprivation to the brain). A milder dose of fear (perhaps meeting your in-laws for the first time) will very likely result in some much milder side-effects, but exactly how we respond to fear stimuli varies greatly from individual to individual.

This is true of audition nerves or fear, and advice on how to deal with fear range from the fairly confusing[1] to the really rather helpful, much of which revolves around 'reframing' the ways in which you perceive and think about the fearful event (an idea we'll look at more closely later in The Toolkit). But, however we cope with our fears, we know that they have a significant effect on our ability to 'be ourselves': to respond naturally to things or to take a risk.

When it comes to giving ourselves directions – such as 'just be yourself' or 'try to respond naturally' – we have even more difficulties to consider. These can be so stubborn that we might want to admit our helplessness in these situations and just leave our minds alone. Here are some typical pieces of audition advice:

- "Please try to come across as a well-adjusted person . . . The casting directors expect you to be pleasant, but don't go overboard."[2]
- "Be truthful and proud to be yourself."[3]

In an ideal world, of course, these little bits of advice would be helpful. That ideal world is the one in which we *know* whether we're coming across as a well-adjusted person, and where we *know* what we're talking about when we say that we're just being ourselves. But our considerations so far must surely convince us that this ideal world isn't the place in which our auditions occur. To add to our confusion we have a strange sort of resistance that happens when we give ourselves directions such as 'be yourself' or 'relax'. This comes about because when we're truly relaxed and are being ourselves it's not because we've told ourselves to. We naturally relax because we are focusing on something that relaxes us (reading, lying on a beach, enjoying dinner with close friends). At such moments, relaxing is the result of a lack of self-consciousness. It's very hard to relax because we tell ourselves to – this is why hypnotists spend so much time getting us to focus on something like falling through clouds or imagining ourselves in a favourite place. Similarly, when we give ourselves directions, these directions can only really be acted upon if we're in a position to receive them. Simple things, like moving your arm to grab a coffee cup will work just fine in most cases. But telling yourself to relax when you're afraid doesn't work because, as we've seen, fear isn't regulated in a part of the brain that is under conscious control.

'Now is the winter of our discontent . . .' line?

Ah, yes. Blanking. Choking. That sudden empty space where the words used to be. We panic, we call for line maybe once, maybe twice; we stumble through apologetically; we're mortified. Of course, the moment we're back out on the street, there they are: 'made glorious summer by this son of York . . .' etc.

Well, we were under pressure. We were having all our usual

audition nerves – surely it is just plain old fear that makes us choke in moments like these? Although the quick answer to that question is 'yes', the fuller and more accurate answer is 'yes, but not always directly'. In other words, it isn't fear directly affecting you and causing you to choke while delivering a song or monologue that you know extremely well (although if you don't know your material well, that's a different story). It's that fear that either: (1) raises your stress levels or (2) encourages you to think about things that don't need thinking about.

In the first case, fear acts as a stressor. If we did not learn our monologue or song under similar stressful conditions, then we are less likely to remember them when we are under stressful conditions. This is called the 'mood-congruity hypothesis'[4] and it has been shown in many research studies that memory works best if you recall things in a mood similar to those in which you learned them. It isn't only mood 'congruency' that aids memory – we are also likely to remember things better if we are back in the place where we laid down the memories. And in a particularly interesting piece of research, it turns out that if we learn a list of words when we're slightly drunk or stoned, we're more likely to remember that list accurately if we are once again drunk or stoned!

So attempting to recall things when you're suddenly in an unfamiliar room and feeling stressed is a challenge and this is one way that fear indirectly affects our susceptibility to 'choking' in audition. This means that in our preparation we would be very wise to think about doing some practice under mildly stressful conditions. As Sian Beilock puts it: 'Practicing under the types of pressures you will face on the big testing day is one of the best ways to combat choking.'[5] This is why drama schools often ask high-profile people in to do mock auditions. However, we need to be able to create strategies for ourselves so that we are able to work under pressure.

The second case is more about the way in which the brain prioritises activity when we're stressed. The brain chemistry of stress is a complex symphony and we don't need to hear all that right now. The important thing for us to know is that our old friend, the amygdala, is involved and it works something like the 'master conductor'. In stressful conditions, the amygdala releases cortisol, which travels down to and disrupts the very area of your brain (the hippocampus) that is busy trying to help you retrieve items from the explicit memory system. Prolonged stress, of course, can have serious effects on memory. But in the short term it can work to disrupt a part of your brain that you were counting on to bring those rehearsal memories to the fore – the result of which is that you momentarily 'blank'.

A third common cause of audition 'choking' is involved with the way in which your brain actually attempts to be as efficient as possible. If you think about what kind of brain-work we need when we first drive a car or first learn a language, you'll be aware that the brain is working very hard indeed. There's a lot of conscious thought going into checking our mirrors, monitoring the space between ourselves and other cars, staying exactly within the speed limits, ensuring that we don't get lost, making a lane change in time, turning on the indicators, avoiding a branch in the road, etc. The list of 'high-resource' brain activity for executing a quick drive down to the shops when we first start driving is impressively long. Of course, once we get more accustomed to driving (or rehearsing a song or monologue), we pass much of this activity into 'low-resource' thinking. We feel as if much of the driving (and rehearsing) that we do becomes somewhat automatic. Our brains need this kind of efficiency in order to process the vast amounts of information that we task them with daily. As we learn, experience and rehearse, we pass large chunks of learned material into the part of our brains that then performs these actions in ways that don't require masses of conscious thought.

Of course, when we're truly prepared for an audition – of the kind that we *can* prepare for – we've done the 'high-resource' intense work of performance. Now most of our material feels as if it's 'in our bones', our music is 'sung in', the words have become 'second nature', we've made and rehearsed our choices over and over: in short, we're able to forget all these details and just concentrate our imaginations so deeply that we can escape the tiny audition room and take ourselves to an imaginary world where we perform with conviction (and, hopefully, brilliance). In a sense, this 'in the bones' feeling is precisely what gives great experts their advantage: much of their performance – whether on a golf course or on stage – involves skill that has passed into 'automaticity' and does not require any spare 'attentional capacity'. No doubt those who master their art or sport manage to get themselves into what Mikhail Czikszentmihalyi has described as the 'flow state': where we feel we're in a special, relaxed and highly focused state of consciousness, undistracted by peripheral things, and trusting the skills we've spent years honing. Of course, stage performance isn't exactly the same as perfecting your tennis backswing into a state of automaticity, but there are similar things that we can achieve in rehearsal – not least of which is the embedding of text, of acting choices, or of technical skills in the automatic memory. When we have that kind of mastery we manage to achieve something extraordinary. Daniel Pink quotes W. H. Auden:

> You need not see what someone is doing
> To know if it is his vocation
>
> You have only to watch his eyes:
> A cook mixing a sauce, a surgeon
>
> Making a primary incision,
> A clerk completing a bill of lading,
>
> Wear the same rapt expression, forgetting
> Themselves in a function.
>
> How beautiful it is,
> The eye-on-the-object look.[6]

Auden's point is important – there is something hypnotic about watching people pursue the things they are really passionate masters of. This, surely, must be another ingredient of the elusive 'it' factor.

When we're not able to get into this 'flow state', however, we often make some fundamental mistakes about how best to think under stress. When we are fearful, or stressed, or nervous, we sometimes think that *more thinking* will improve what we're doing. So we start to think about things we don't need to think about any more. But the trouble with this kind of last-minute, nerve- or fear-inspired thinking is that it gets done with the wrong part of the brain. Highly complex skills actually require *implicit* rather than *explicit* control for their execution – in other words, highly complex skills are executed by a part of the brain that you don't control consciously. This means that in order to perform well in a stressful situation, you must *leave your mind alone*. You must trust the unconscious controller to execute what it learned in those hours and hours of practice to perfect your golf swing, your tennis stroke, your high C, your incredibly complex and compelling reading of Hamlet. You must *not* think about it consciously as you execute it, because if you do you'll be switching from the part of your mind that stores and operates your expertise to the 'attentional' part of your mind that you used when you first learned the skill. In other words: if you think consciously about things that you have rehearsed into a state of expertise, you will suddenly find yourself back in the state you were in when you first learned the skill.

Anyone who is a good touch-typist will tell you that thinking about your fingers and where they go when you type will seriously impair your typing accuracy. If you're an experienced and expert touch-typist, you never use that conscious part of your brain to direct your fingers – you stopped doing that long ago. Not only do you have to leave your mind alone, you have to *trust* it. And you can trust it, if you've put in the right amount of work and learned your material in the right way. This is the point where getting to a place of 'mastery' is so critical.

Of course, when we're in a high-stress situation where we're trying to do our best it's not uncommon to lose that sense of trust and to decide that thinking about stuff we already have down pat will help us. For the very same reason that we often remember things when we stop trying, we will often lose lines when we are. This is the point at which having a secure mental process is similarly critical.

Auditions create the perfect conditions for inspiring fear, for making us choke and for causing us to think when we absolutely don't need to. In the second section of this book we'll be looking very specifically at how we might begin to wage our own little war against these conditions and find some practical ways through all the side-effects of a heavy dose of fear. Along with battling our fears, we need to look at what part dedication and commitment play in building our audition master plan.

5 THE HARD WORK OF GENIUS

I've often heard audition panel members talk about the way in which an actor has or (more often) hasn't 'mastered' their material. I routinely tell young actor/singers that I work with that they're not ready to audition if they haven't mastered their material. Often, when working under the tight conditions of weekly live television shows I counsel singers quickly between takes: 'Don't let the song sing *you*'. It has to be the other way around. Many MDs I know express this by saying that a song 'isn't sung in yet'. These are all shorthand ways of saying that the material isn't ready to perform. But what does it really mean to 'master' audition material, or to feel that a song is 'sung in' or isn't 'singing you'? What does it take to master a monologue from *Love's Labours Lost* and how does that mastery compare with the kind of work it takes to master chess, ballet, tennis or musical composition?

At a glance that comparison might sound absurd. I've known actors with three or four years of training and experience who manage to convince an audition panel that they are at the top of their game and capable of working at a professional level in a tough and competitive industry. But I can't help wondering how that compares with what people who study excellence and outstanding human achievement in areas like sport or music have come to see as the 'ten-year, 10,000-hour' rule.

Falling on your butt 20,000 times

It's become commonplace in books like Malcolm Gladwell's *Outliers*, Matthew Syed's *Bounce* and Daniel Coyle's *The Talent Code*, to consider the question of exactly what it takes to master something. The answer appears to be: 10,000 hours or ten years. In a very real sense, the idea underlying this answer is that it turns out that talent isn't necessarily a 'you either have it or you don't' sort of proposition. According to Gladwell, the 10,000-hour/ten-year rule can be traced in many areas of 'genius'. He cites, among others, The Beatles (who, having performed many hours in Hamburg between the years of 1960 and 1964, met the 10,000-hour mark) and Bill Gates, who started programming computers at the age of thirteen. While it might be hard to convince us that the particular brilliance of The Beatles or Gates is all simply down to the hours they put in, research certainly suggests that there's something extraordinary to be said for this kind of long and dedicated practice. Daniel Coyle's book looks very specifically at the way in which the right kind of practice works on the brain's plasticity (a complicated tale about building a myelin layer that works like a sort of neuro 'superconductor') and actually creates the right neurological conditions for excellence. Matthew Syed sees the time requirement for mastery as part of the 'hidden logic' of success:

> So the question is: How long do you need to practise in order to achieve excellence? Extensive research, it turns out, has come up with a very specific answer to that question: from art to science and from board games to tennis, it has been found that a minimum of ten years is required to reach world-class status in any complex task . . . What the science is telling us is that many thousands of hours of practice are necessary to break into the realm of excellence.[1]

It seems that there is a fair amount of agreement on this, although I am sure that in the arts there is still much research to do in order to be absolutely sure that certain innate skills and abilities don't come into play. For the moment the rallying cry among those who write books with titles like *Talent Is Overrated* is that what we've generally taken for 'genius' actually turns out to be just plain old hard work. There are many examples cited in these books, most of which are hard to refute. But suppose we take this idea as a given and try to think of it in terms of the auditioning performer. Can we really talk about acting 'mastery' or 'genius' in this way? Can we really imagine actors putting in ten years or 10,000 hours in order to achieve a kind of 'mastery' or excellence in their craft? We can certainly imagine these things applying in other areas of the performing arts, like music or dance, and some would even put visual arts into this frame.[2] But could we ever convince ourselves that actors may need a similar ten-year dedication to their craft in order to attain excellence or world-class status in their field?

Well, the immediate answer might be 'no', since many of us have known performers who just seem like naturals, possessed of a genius of some mysterious origin. But might it be that it only *seems* this way to us? Certainly, most of us also know the way in which really seasoned performers can cope with challenging situations in a manner that eludes the novice, but does doing eight shows a week for ten years really result in a kind of mastery? Well, if scientific studies are correct, it *might* – *if* the performer was consciously pushing the boundaries of their capabilities at each and every performance. This idea of 'deep practice' or 'dedicated practice' is one that researchers say is what lies behind the building of excellence over the course of the ten years. Essentially, the idea behind 'deep practice' is that a person must continually work at the very edge of their capabilities, make errors, correct the errors and resist the urge to simply repeat what is already coming pretty easily. This – as those of us who have done an extended run of a show know – is not the way in which most actors work on a long run. Indeed, muddling through in a state of 'automaticity' is more likely the norm in the West End and on Broadway. The same holds true for singers: I've often served on panels where performers are described (and then dismissed) as 'club singers' or 'am dram', essentially meaning that (along with some questionable taste in their performance) they tend to sing or act as if on autopilot.

But let's imagine that we could work for ten years, doing eight shows a week, consciously concentrating on pushing the boundaries of our capabilities at each and every performance. What might that mean? Let's imagine this by supposing that I've just landed a part in an extended run of *Twelfth Night*. I could decide for any given performance that I'll concentrate on finding a greater breadth of 'musicality' in my speaking voice and finer internal sense of rhythm with the verse. Or perhaps the next night I might concentrate on elicit-ing a new or subtly different response from an actor that I'm playing a scene with. Of course these aims must be simultaneously achieved while maintaining a profound sense of belief and a vividly imagined sense of the world around me and, indeed, must be pursued in ways that deepen rather than diminish my commitment to that imagined world. Certainly, we could come up with any number of areas to concentrate on in our quest to use every performance as an oppor-tunity to push the boundaries of our expressive capabilities as an actor.

Now let us imagine that we do this for every performance we give (whether it's *Twelfth Night* or singing for club or 'function' gigs) over the next ten years. Would it not be likely that (if the feedback received from directors, fellow actors and musicians, and audiences tells us that we're on the right track) at the end of ten years of this concentrated effort we would indeed be justifiably able to describe ourselves as masters of performance? Might our performances even have some-thing of 'genius' about them? At the very least, would we not have a tremendous confidence in our ability and an extraordinarily enhanced sense of heightened awareness on stage and deepened imagination?

We'll probably never know the answer to these questions because it's unlikely that any of us would ever have the patience to follow and document ten years of such practice. But we might ponder why it is that when this ten-year 'deep practice' model is suggested for a ballet dancer or a concert pianist we can imagine it so much more easily. We expect that ballet dancers or concert pianists need years of a certain kind of practice that leads them to mastery, but we don't necessarily see that kind of mastery as analogous to excellence in acting. It is almost certainly true that it takes many years of acting to realise that acting is difficult and this is one of the marvellous paradoxes of our work. Everyone knows, even at the start, that becoming a great dancer or a great violinist is going to be very difficult, but most people think acting is easy. It isn't until you gain much more experience that you truly realise that your first assessment was made in ignorance. This truth is brought home to me in a quotation from Ellen Terry: 'Only a great actor finds the difficulties of the actor's art infinite' and one from Glenda Jackson: 'The more you [act], the more you realise how painfully easy it is to be lousy, and how very difficult to be good'. So perhaps we start off with the idea that acting is pretty simple and doesn't require much skill, and then don't always fully adjust our views as we go along.

I rehearse all this only to make the point that there are very few performers I know who think about how they might approach something like mastery or excellence when it comes to acting. I've seen people take songs and monologues into auditions that they've learned the night before (although, of course, there are times when the audition itself requires this kind of work). The great majority of auditioning actors/performers have had a few years of very sporadic experience in secondary school or youth theatre, followed by three years in a drama school. If they've been lucky, perhaps roughly half of their tutors/directors have done more good than harm in their development, and once they've left drama school they are often performing *only* during those five to ten minutes of audition perhaps five or six times a month.

Is it time for us to start taking the idea of mastery a little more seriously as actors? Is it time to start looking at what practising in a more dedicated and challenging way could do for our careers?

Research into the world of figure skating has revealed that what separates elite skaters from the rest of the pack lies in the level of difficulty they attempt in practice. In other words, the elite skaters continually practise things just *beyond* their capabilities much more often. The consequence of this, of course, is that the elite skaters fall far more often than the merely proficient skaters. Geoff Colvin, writing about Olympic skater Shizuka Arakawa, estimated that she fell more than 20,000 times from the age of five until the 2006 Olympics. As he concludes: 'Landing on your butt twenty thousand times is where great performance comes from.'[3]

Arts and crafts

What kind of skills can auditioning performers reasonably hope to bring up to the level of expertise that Colvin and others talk about when citing the ten-year/10,000-hour rule? Certainly, we don't have the sort of practice routines that golfers or tennis players or even pianists have. What could be reasonably tackled if we made the decision that we were going to hit that time requirement for the label of expertise? For singers and dancers, the practice skills seem obvious. But for actors, at first glance, it seems a lot tougher to define. Acting just isn't like tennis: a motor skill like a great backhand swing is not comparable to the complexity of playing Hamlet. True enough, they are very different skills when compared this way. But perhaps we might feel differently about that comparison if we were to break core acting skills down into specific components. What does it take to play Hamlet? We may all have our own list, but for the sake of argument I'll put this one forth:

1. Physical strength
2. Vocal strength, flexibility, variety
3. Expressive range: a both subtle and bold expressive 'palette'
4. Ability to comprehend and express complex thought
5. Strength/depth of imagination
6. Strength of empathetic/emotional sensibility

Of course, the things on this list are only 'academically' separable: in the practice of acting they overlap. One and two are closely related to three, and four to six are bound into each other in the very act of playing Hamlet. But still, in this 'component' form, we can begin to imagine how we might formulate a regular and disciplined plan of practice. However, most actors I know either feel that they can't do much on their own, or simply don't bother. They feel that they need a class or a rehearsal in order to work on their skills. Is this the reason, perhaps, that it would never occur to many actors that they should be putting in the kind of hours that Andy Murray, Darcey Bussell or Kiri Te Kanawa might? Why is it that, compared with athletes, dancers or musicians, actors are – in the main – an incredibly 'unpractised' lot?

Imagine Picasso or Yo-Yo Ma claiming that they can't work without an audience or a class. Of course that sounds absurd. First of all, surely a visual artist shouldn't be concerned at all with their 'audience', should they? Artists should be concerned with their art, with how it expresses their particular view of the world, and with how they can visually render that view. They don't need audiences. Yo-Yo Ma needs to attain a level of virtuosity that gives his particular interpretation of a cello concerto an excitement and a 'point of view' that lesser players can't attain. We expect that both of these artists will spend hours on their own in a studio of some kind, but we don't expect this of actors. We say instead that acting is collaborative, that the 'whole' needs its many parts working together and that actors can't 'interact' on their own. But isn't the flip side of this argument to imagine that Picasso *didn't* collaborate with the world that he sees around him? That he didn't 'interact' with this world? That Yo-Yo Ma doesn't work collaboratively with a conductor and an orchestra to create the 'magic' of his concerto? The more we question, the clearer it becomes that we seem somehow to see acting as discipline that is very unlike any other, and that what we expect from a dancer or a musician is not what we expect from an actor.

Maybe, fundamentally, we just don't take acting very seriously. Because until we're ready to accept that it requires the same kind of dedication and time that other disciplines do, we'll always think it's acceptable to go into audition with pieces we just haven't mastered and skills that just aren't perfected.

Realism and the 'garret' attitude

Actors often look to directors for answers. As a director, of course, there are many times when I'm happy to oblige, particularly in the early phases of rehearsal when we're all still trying to articulate and understand a particular vision of a piece. But there are probably just as many times – especially in the later phases of rehearsal – when I think it's important to encourage actors to search for the answers themselves. This is not a question of laziness (like most directors I like to make decisions), but rather a question of the ways in which actors take ownership of their work when the ideas they're using came from a tough process of working things out for themselves. I can think of many times in rehearsal when I've responded to an actor's question with: 'You're the artist here, what do you think'? I always sense that applying the term 'artist' to an actor doesn't necessarily sit easily with what it is, exactly, that actors think they are. This might be because, unlike Picasso, actors are generally not the originator of work. They are the interpreters of work. But that certainly doesn't compromise the idea of being an artist: we wouldn't deny that a great interpretation of Beckett or Mozart is an art. Yet, we can't imagine many actors adopting some sort of 'garret' attitude, in which they pursue what they think to be their artistic ideals – beauty, truth, symmetry, provocation, grit, fantasy, the unexpected, etc. – no matter what others may think. Fundamentally, of course, this is because whereas painting and poetry are expected to be solitary artistic pursuits, acting is a collaborative one. The maverick, the visionary theatre artist, is generally thought to be the director. This has always meant that, for many, the actor is expected to be subservient to the director's vision, and therefore it isn't hard to understand why actors are uncomfortable with the idea of their 'craft' being elevated to the description of 'art'.

But I can't help wondering, as we contemplate the importance of hard work and of taking acting seriously, if this distinction has led us into some pretty self-defeating behaviour, not least of which is the often over-developed desire to please. Actors seem happy striving to please directors, teachers and audition panels, but are often less concerned about striving to please *themselves* in terms of their own artistic standards. Is that because we don't routinely think about these standards? Is that why actors simply don't tend to have that bloody-minded, starving artist attitude that insists on creating art that is true to one's vision – whether the public (or casting directors) like it or not?

I couldn't begin to count the number of times when, doing an audition workshop, someone asks me: 'What are you looking for in an audition?' It's got to be the most common question in these kinds of sessions. I've headed many training programmes where I brought in guest directors, casting directors and agents and always they get the question. As strange as it may sound, I think the answer for nearly everyone I know who auditions performers for a living is the same:

they want *you* to show them what they're looking for. They want *you* to show them what you're all about, what you'll do in this role that no one else can do. They want *you* to show them what your art is all about: inspiration, muscular imagination, surprising and wholly committed ideas and expression, faultless technique and superb, illuminating interpretation.

Of course, this sounds like an impossible answer, but then it's an impossible question. However, if there is any answer then this is it. There is no secret, and unless we're willing to work toward all of the things described above, there's no other serious advice available. If you aim to achieve mastery and to better your performance in each audition you do, you just might find that pleasing others isn't as important as pleasing yourself, and being your own master.

Learning to serve

It never fails to discourage me when I see 'how-to-audition' books with chapter or section titles like: 'Thank you. Next' or 'We'll Call *You*' or, indeed, entire books with titles like *Thank You, That's All We Need for Today*. As an actor reading these it makes my position in the whole picture *very* clear: I am disposable, I am one of hundreds, I am nothing special. Is this really what an ethical and intelligent audition panel member/casting director wants me to feel? Of course, these books – despite their titles – mean to be helpful. These same books will go on to tell us how we must be confident, be professional, be sure of ourselves, etc., but honestly – are we likely to feel that when we read these kinds of chapter headings or titles? In the interest of fairness, of course, these authors are simply trying to make us be realistic. They are trying to make us understand the simple fact that power in the audition situation lies in the hands of the auditioning panel, and that what they say goes if you want to find work: if you want that part, and you've done your audition, when the panel say 'thank you, next', don't hang about – scuttle out the door politely and be *realistic*. It's absolutely realistic to do as you're told if you want to get the job, isn't it?

Well, that's an interesting question, because being realistic about our dreams is surely a self-defeating exercise. If we have any experience at all in this business, we know that our chances of making a living in it are very slim indeed. We know that many of us will audition for years with little or no success despite the fact that we've trained, been assured by our tutors that we're pretty good at what we do, and (we think) we know how to conduct ourselves professionally at an audition. But we also know that in order to get up in the morning and get to that next audition, we *can't* be wholly realistic. In fact it is absolutely essential to our success that we *aren't*.

Auditioning is what games-theory folk would call a zero-sum game, which means that a person can only win if everyone else loses. In that sense, auditioning performers are in the same position that athletes are in, but their situation is even more acute. When we audition, we don't get a bronze medal for third place. In fact, as a general rule, we don't even find out if we *were* third place. So that makes the 'zero' part of the 'zero-sum' game of auditioning even more intense. Furthermore, we all know that when it comes to auditioning we're in the toughest zero-sum competition of our lives as actors. However, athletes are well ahead of us in terms of having a much more extensive library of sport psychology books and research to help bolster performance under this kind of pressure. For this reason I'm always interested in catching up with whatever is recent and relevant in the area of enhancing sports performance under pressure. For example, something Matthew Syed calls 'Irrational Optimism' seems to be critical to sports performance success:

> World-class performers . . . have taught themselves to ratchet up their optimism at the point of performance; to mould the evidence to fit their beliefs rather than the other way around; to activate doublethink. And it is proficiency in these skills that often separate the best from the rest. Muhammad Ali, Jonathan Edwards, Tiger Woods, Arsène Wenger, Nick Faldo: all, in their different ways, have found an irrational way to triumph.[4]

Syed's point is that in order to perform at a high level we can't take our zero-sum worries into performance with us. We can't think about the odds against us winning, we can't concentrate on the very real fact that our last four or five auditions have resulted in rejection, we can't think about how many other people are waiting in the room to go in before or after us, we can't call up Equity and find out just how many of their members are 'resting' at any given time – we can only carry in our dreams of winning. Finding this crucial balance between realism and an irrational belief in ourselves is an absolute requirement for surviving and even winning in the battle of the audition room. We know this, but we don't spend time thinking about how to achieve it.

We simply don't have the kinds of resources that athletes do when they look around for inspiration and advice on the mental toughness needed to win. While there are 'performance psychologists' who specialise in the arts, they are far less easy to find than the legion of sports psychologists. A quick trawl of the Amazon website is particularly revealing. Under a search for 'sports psychology' you get 5,314 results, and titles on the first page include: *Ahead of the Game: How to Use Your Mind to Win in Sport*, and *Mind Games: Inspirational Lessons from the World's Finest Sports Stars*. Under a search for 'performing arts psychology', you get 1,117 results, and titles on the first page include: *Physical and Emotional Hazards of a Performing Career* and *Advice for Dancers: Emotional Counsel and Practical Strategies*. This captures the different approaches in a nutshell: the sports folk are focusing on positive mind strategies and the performing arts folk are looking at damage limitation. There just doesn't seem to be much in the way of helpful winning mental strategies for performing artists, and in the absence of these 'off-the-shelf' experts we turn to 'how-to-audition' books or to those who train us. Maybe it's time to look further afield.

Professional Preparation 101

Yes, we all do them. Those of us who write actor-training curricula and those who go through it know the obligatory final-year class which inevitably involves talks from Equity folk, a friendly tax accountant, some recent school successes who've had their arm gently twisted into coming back and sharing their experiences with the young about-to-be-turned-out-into-the-profession students, and lectures on how to prepare for audition, write letters and CVs, get an agent and prepare for an agent's showcase. They are necessary classes that hope to bridge the educational experience and the professional environment. But are those of us who plan and deliver them getting it right? Are we delivering enough in terms of mental strategies, winning attitudes and advice on coping? I've been responsible for managing classes like these for more than two decades and I don't remember anyone talking about mental strategies or winning attitudes, so I suppose the question of whether we were getting it right in this area is moot. However, the one thing we do tend to stress in these classes is the importance of being *realistic*. There's a lot of talk generally about the importance of recognising that this is a tough business and that very few actually make a living in it, and lots of statistical evidence about how fewer than 5 per cent of all actors manage to make a living out of acting alone. Yes, it's tough. And young people going out into the industry need to face that.

Maybe the reality of it all is sobering, but performing artists aren't alone in entering a tough field. Fashion designers, artists, architects, classical musicians, athletes and many others face that same reality check. For example, here's what the US Bureau of Labor Statistics has to say about the chances of making a living as an athlete:

> Few people who dream of becoming paid professional athletes, *coaches*, or sports officials beat the odds and make a full-time living from professional athletics. Professional athletes often have short careers with little job security. Even though the chances of employment as a professional athlete are slim, there are many opportunities for at least a part-time job as a coach, instructor, referee, or umpire in amateur athletics or in high school, college, or university sports.[5]

Of course you could easily substitute the word *actors, directors* or *producers* for the '*athletes, coaches,* or *sports officials*' above, and come to exactly the same conclusions, so why do athletes seem to have so much more at their disposal in terms of mental strategies and coping techniques? Why is it that in our Professional Preparation 101 classes we tend to harp on about the difficulties of the profession instead gathering everyone together and encouraging them to work on their positive mental outlook? One simple answer might be that athletes have very specific markers of attainment. You either can or can't run the 100 metres in under ten seconds. You either can or can't do a triple toe loop. Given this empirical certainty, it's so much easier to see when a particular kind of mental approach is having a positive effect. It's a lot harder to see how specific 'cognitive reframing' techniques might enhance your rendition of Lady Macbeth. So perhaps that lack of research and popular techniques is simply the result of the 'immeasurability' of a great performance in the world of acting. However, this still doesn't entirely explain why we dwell on the negative so much.

The more I consider the questions regarding how seriously we take our work as performing artists, how much time we're willing to dedicate to mastering our discipline, how often we happily take the subservient role, and how little time we spend getting our mental attitude just right for peak performance, the less surprising it seems that I've spent hours in audition rooms watching the silly, the unprepared and the defeated go through the motions.

But I'm still not convinced that the answer to improving audition performance is going to be found in audition 'how-to' books, or even in conventional training courses. The answer has to be in taking performing seriously. The answer has to be connected with knowing just how difficult it is to master material, and what kind of dedication it takes to perform with confidence and focus. If we go back to consider what sports psychology research suggests, there is some clear agreement on what it takes to be a master athlete. Sports psychologist Graham Jones has made an exhaustive study of the habits and attitudes of great athletes, and concludes that along with hours and hours of dedicated practice, what distinguishes a great athlete is *mental toughness*. According to Graham's research, athletes who possess mental toughness have:

1. An unshakeable belief in their ability
2. The ability to bounce back after a loss or setback

3. An unshakeable belief in their own unique qualities, which put them ahead of others
4. An insatiable, intrinsic motivation to keep at it
5. The ability to stay fully focused in the face of distraction
6. The ability to regain psychological control in the face of the unexpected
7. The ability to push back the boundaries of pain or distress in the midst of competition
8. An acceptance of anxiety as part of competition and strategies for coping with it
9. A distance that allows them not to be affected by the performance of others
10. A spirit that thrives on competition
11. The ability to maintain focus through personal life distractions
12. The ability to switch performance focus on and off[6]

I don't know a single performer who wouldn't be infinitely better off with that kind of mental toughness. Athletes achieve this, so surely we can.

Summary

In this section we've looked at the relationship between confidence and hard work, and between confidence and mental preparation. We've considered the importance of being mentally tough, and we know that this mental toughness goes hand-in-hand with the kind of confidence that comes from long hours of dedicated practice. No matter how we look at it, we have to keep coming back to the question: How much time and dedication are performers willing to put into mastering their craft and are they ready to take performing seriously enough to dedicate themselves in this way? The only way in which you could imagine any performers doing so, would be if that performer had point number four above: an insatiable, intrinsic sense of motivation.

In the last chapter of this section, before we begin the work of building a strategy for truly mastering auditions, we need to consider where motivation comes from, how it is linked to the ability to discipline ourselves and just how serious we are when we talk about our love of performing.

6 WHAT'S MY MOTIVATION?

There are many reasons why people audition and these reasons are always associated with various other goals: from getting into acting school, to getting a job to pay the rent, to getting onto a reality television show. But if you were to ask yourself the question: 'Why am I auditioning?' in a more general sense, what would your answer be?

For most people reading this book, I'm guessing that it's something you do pretty regularly and that it's part of your overall career plan. You may be at an early stage in your career and having spent some time training and you now want to put that training to good use. It may be that you love performing and you want the opportunity to do it regularly. Or perhaps it is something fairly new to you and it might be that you just want to see how a professional panel respond to you. It might be that you want to prove something to yourself or to others. There are hundreds of reasons why people audition, and no doubt they do so without a kind of specific long-term goal in mind.

For many reasons knowing what motivates us to audition and to perform, and having some larger sense of purpose in our heads when we do, really matters. The ability to articulate what it is that is driving our desire to keep performing and auditioning is a critical one and it makes a significant difference in terms of how long we can bring ourselves to take the inevitable knock-backs in the audition game. It matters even more in terms of how long we can bring ourselves to do some dedicated and meaningful practice, even when we haven't been in school or had a performing job for months. Indeed, at these times we need to practise more than ever because there's absolutely no structure in place to focus our work: no director, no opening night, and no class to get up for in the morning. At these moments it's all down to motivation: it's all about how we keep going when it's just ourselves and our desire to be the absolute best we can be and to confidently face the challenge of beating every other candidate in every audition we go to.

Surely we couldn't even begin to consider doing this kind of work if we weren't motivated. But motivation to keep practising is something that eludes a lot of 'resting' performers and at these moments we have to question what influences us: What makes us want to be in this business and have the heart to face its volatility and obvious unfairness, its overall lack of reasonable compensation for the hours we put into it and even its mind-numbing repetitiveness (in the eight-shows-a-week West End experience)? I've spent many years listening to fellow panel members asking some young hopeful why they want to be an actor or a singer (I no longer bother to ask this question) and hearing the answer 'It's what I've always wanted to do. I can't see myself doing anything else'. This is far and away the most common answer to this question, but I think it's a very unsatisfactory way to explain *what* is motivating us to be actors and performers and *why* we put ourselves through it in the first place.

The question is not trivial. The general 'It's all I've ever seen myself doing' responses simply won't serve, because unless we can manage to identify and harness our motivation we're never going to demonstrate the kind of 'mastery' and confidence that the 'how-to-audition' books tell us are critical to success in this business.

Dreaming the impossible dream

Perhaps more important than wondering why you audition is an even bigger question: Why have you chosen performing arts as a profession in the first place? The standard interview answers – 'It's the only thing I've ever seen myself doing' or 'It's the only thing I'm really passionate about' – cleverly avoid and simultaneously raise the more difficult issues, such as: Why aren't you passionate about other things? Why haven't you ever seen yourself doing anything else? Acting, unlike dancing or 100-metre hurdling, requires that we work creatively in ensembles to develop and tell a story, and that we take on the persona of others and get right inside their skins. How could we possibly do these things well if we aren't passionately curious about human behaviour and psychology; about how our art differs from and fits alongside other arts (like visual arts) in the pursuit of telling stories, or about the power of language and literature? Surely these fundamental questions demonstrate why great performing demands that we be passionate about a lot of other things besides performing. But what motivates that passion?

For some researchers who specialise in motivation, the answers to these questions come down to whether you could be classified as someone who is motivated by achievement or someone who is motivated by the fear of failure. There has been some interesting research into the relationship between fear and motivation and between achievement and motivation. It seems that success, and the kinds of goals we set for ourselves, are closely linked to whether we are motivated by: (1) the expectation of achievement (the belief that if we set reasonable, challenging goals we can – with sufficient work and perseverance – meet them); or (2) the fear of failure (the expectation that we are not likely to succeed). Robert Kelsey – a self-confessed lifelong 'fear of failure' type – describes research into this area, which found that:

> an individual's performance was dictated by whether they had high or low levels of innate 'achievement motivation' . . . those with high achievement motivation levels [were] driven by their expectations regarding the payoff of task fulfilment, and those with low achievement motivation levels [were] motivated to avoid [certain tasks] due to an anticipation, or fear, of failure.[1]

This research concluded that those with high achievement motivation (High-AMs) pursued a range of averagely to highly demanding tasks because they were focused on the reward of success. Those with the high fear of failure (High-FFs) displayed anxiety about intermediate tasks and in some cases chose to avoid them entirely. But as Kelsey points out, the research resulted in one more startling discovery, which I think is of some interest to us:

High-FFs had no problem attempting tasks that were deemed very difficult or almost impossible. This was due to the fact that the price of failure was reduced. So while High-AMs chose a challenging but achievable range of tasks in anticipation of success and reward, High-FFs chose only those tasks they were almost certain to complete or almost certain to fail.[2]

So it seems that people motivated by achievement thrive on a challenge that is well-matched to their abilities and their commitment level. But those who are motivated by their fear of failure tend to choose things that are either too simple (so of course they will succeed) or too hard (so that expectation of success would be unrealistic). The question that comes to my mind is this: Are some of us choosing a tough profession because success in this field is a pretty unrealistic outcome?

In his book *Destructive Goal Pursuit*, D. Christopher Kayes relates the tragic story of a team of Mt Everest climbers who defied all reason and doggedly pursued their goals in the face of depleted oxygen and dangerous, quickly turning weather. He observes that the climbers were so single-minded in accomplishing their task that they failed to adapt to the rapidly changing circumstances around them. Kayes concludes that it was this inflexibility that cost them their lives. Kayes puts his case carefully, however, as most research demonstrates that goal setting is generally a very positive thing: something that we can probably conclude for ourselves without the help of research. But how can we be certain that our own goals are constructive and likely to lead to positive outcomes? According to Kayes there are some strong indicators that warn of potentially destructive patterns in goal setting:

1. *Narrowly defined goals*: goals that are too specific and too narrow usually lead to problems 'when conditions require learning'. Narrow goals make it hard to adapt to new/different circumstances.
2. *Weight of public expectation*: this can lead us to stick with goals if abandonment might be perceived by others as failure.

3. *Face-saving behaviour*: this occurs when the goal-pursuer seeks to maintain identity even in the face of contradictory evidence. The goal-seeker wants to maintain a public 'persona' even when achievement becomes far less certain and results in anxiety.

4. *Idealised future*: an over-idealised notion of the future may provide motivation and hope, but taken to extremes it can blind the goal-seeker to the reality of both present and possible alternative futures.

5. *Goal-driven justification*: when the pursuit of a goal is justified simply because it is a goal, which is what gets so many of the Everest climbers in trouble.

6. *Associating a goal with 'destiny'*: encouraging the idea that somehow, in some 'cosmic' way we are destined to achieve something, rather than considering alternatives.[3]

These indicators are helpful but they also complicate the picture for us. We know that the only way to really get things done is to have a sense of direction: to know where you're going. But Kayes raises a significant point that can be seen pretty clearly in certain areas, such as climbing Everest and, perhaps, trying to win *The X Factor*, break into Hollywood or get into the West End. What is the point at which the over-pursuit of goals becomes a kind of 'blind driver' that leaves you inflexible and scared of turning back or rethinking? I've known many performers for whom this is a huge issue. In these cases the performer's drive is a bit like the gambler's: the next roll could be the big one.

The key to keeping our goals positive, I think, must be in keeping them broad enough to cover changes in direction and conditions, and also in learning to recognise when we're idealising, rationalising, face-saving or responding to external pressure or expectation. We also need to think deeply about whether we've chosen a particular (nearly impossible) goal because it softens the blow if we don't manage to achieve it. In other words, for people who are highly motivated by the fear of failure it's easier to attempt to climb Mt Everest than it is to attempt to increase your running distance. This is because, with hard work and persistence, you can always increase your running distance.

Therefore not doing so clearly means that you either have specific physical limitations, or else you just didn't put in the effort and you failed to achieve a relatively simple (if challenging) task. Climbing Mt Everest, however, is a monumental task that is attempted by a relative few, and failure is likely to be judged kindly because in such a daunting task, failure is a probable (and 'forgivable') outcome.

Does it matter if we're being driven into an impossible goal out of fear? There's no science here to fall back on, but my argument is that it does, if only in terms of our own happiness. Of course, this doesn't mean you shouldn't set goals, but it does mean that you have to define them carefully and make sure that you're always striving for multiple indicators of success. It also means that we might be in a better position to set those goals if we know whether we're motivated by fear or achievement.

Perhaps, when we're thinking about all the various things that have motivated us in our choice of a performing career, it might be important to consider where we fall on the 'High-AM' to 'High-FF' spectrum. Is it possible that this is one other element in a long list of things that we don't really know about ourselves? Is it time to start asking some more probing questions about what has really motivated us to go in this direction in the first place?

On the limitations of carrots and sticks

Other recent research into motivation has proved both surprising and fascinating, and is well worth considering in the context of performing. Daniel H. Pink, the author of *Drive: The Surprising Truth about What Motivates Us*, has looked closely at the whole business of what drives us and is careful to distinguish between two different types of motivation: extrinsic and intrinsic. Extrinsic motivation, as you might have guessed, is all about external reward for your effort. That could come in the form of a bonus, higher pay or a prize of some sort for a given kind of behaviour, or indeed, even the promise of a leading role on Broadway. For many years management theories and theories about people's behaviour in general have embraced the idea that extrinsic motivation drives us to greater performance. This is the whole purpose behind a fund manager's big bonus or other kinds of performance-related pay. The idea seems logical enough: a big carrot of some sort, dangling off the end of stick right in front of you, is bound to motivate you to move faster and be better. But these days there's serious doubt about this idea, and that doubt is based on some significant research. Pink concludes that there are 'Seven Deadly Flaws' to the work-for-reward syndrome. The problem is with rewards is that:

1. They can extinguish intrinsic motivation
2. They can diminish performance
3. They can crush creativity
4. They can crowd out good behaviour
5. They can encourage cheating, shortcuts and unethical behaviour
6. They can become addictive
7. They can foster short-term thinking[4]

In a common-sense way, we think we understand the relationship between reward and behaviour: the greater the reward, the greater the effort. But the surprising truth is that greater reward (and however much effort we may put in to attain it) creates more unreliable results, and in some cases really big rewards are downright counterproductive. The hard facts are that extrinsic motivations in the form of big rewards can lead to some fairly negative outcomes, not least that big rewards can distract us. They can switch our focus from what drives us internally to what might be 'in it for us', they can encourage short-term thinking, they can (if the reward is large enough) encourage some terrible behaviour – just look at the temptations and the disasters of the recent high bonuses for selling poor (or 'sub-prime') financial products – and they can refocus our thinking in ways that aren't helpful or creative when it comes to solving specific problems. And these are only *some* of the problems of extrinsic motivators.

Author Dan Ariely recounts an experiment in India (the only place where his relatively modest grant money would support his experiment) in which local workers were offered anywhere from the equivalent of one day's worth to five months' worth of salary if they could perform well in some chosen tasks. The researchers were surprised at the results:

> Those who stood to earn the most demonstrated the lowest level of performance. Relative to those in the low- or medium-bonus conditions, they achieved good or very good performance less than a third of the time. The experience was so stressful to those in the very-large-bonus condition that they choked under the pressure.[5]

This will sound familiar to actors who have auditioned for a potentially life-changing role, only to find themselves freezing up with fear at the thought of what was at stake and how important it was to them. In another study, researchers found that extrinsic reward for work can lead to either narrow focus or self-censoring. A group of painters were asked to randomly select some of their paintings that they had been paid to do (commissioned work) and some of their paintings that they were not paid to do (non-commissioned work). The paintings were then displayed to a panel of experts and curators who were asked to rate the paintings on both creativity and technical skill. Again the results were surprising: 'The commissioned works were rated as significantly less creative than the non-commissioned works, yet they were not rated as different in technical quality.'[6] The inevitable conclusion is that the paintings the artists thought they were doing just for themselves, for the pure joy of painting, were better works of art.

When is it work?

One of the big problems with extrinsic rewards for work is that it can take what we often find to be an intrinsic joy in engaging in a particular activity and turns it into ... well ... *work*. And once we're *working* we generally have an entirely different way of viewing what we're doing.

Most auditioning performers are doing some form of work that pays the bills (and which may or may not in itself be rewarding), but they're also working incredibly hard at another job – auditioning – that they do for free. And that 'free' work puts enormous pressure on them. If we're not being compensated, then what are we doing it *for*? The longer we stay in this situation, the more critical it is that we can make it pay off.

However, most performers are happy to take on this free work. They invest money and emotion and time into a series of speculative events that may not pay off. Most manage to keep going because this speculative activity has a meaning, and finding meaning in our work is critical to motivation. This idea was tested recently in an interesting way by a team who set a group of volunteers a challenge: to build Lego Bionicles for a small amount of money[7]. The building of the Bionicles was not important in itself, what the team were trying to discover was how the volunteers would react to the ways in which their completed Bionicles were treated. After completion, one group's Bionicles were simply accepted by the researcher on duty, and the volunteer builder was paid a very modest sum of money and given another Bionicle to build. The other group, however, had a more disheartening experience. When their Bionicle was completed the 'duty researcher' paid them, gave them a second box of Bionicle parts to put together, and made sure that the volunteer could see them begin to completely dismantle the Bionicle they'd just built. In this second situation, the volunteers quickly became aware that as soon as they built their robot it was going to be destroyed. You can probably guess the results of the experiment: the volunteer builders who could see their work immediately dismantled lost interest in the project and gave up much more quickly than the builders whose work was simply accepted without being destroyed. Both were offered the same amount of money to build, so the only difference was that in the first case the builders could imagine some point to their work, whereas in the second, the builders were immediately aware that the work itself was pointless.

So what can a story about Bionicles tell us about auditioning? Well, it is a sad reality of the business that as auditioning performers we are, in a sense, 'building Bionicles' for free. In fact, auditioning usually *costs* something: the time you give up in preparation, the money it costs to transport yourself there and the afternoon you take off work to go. In the case of actors who attend many auditions over the course of their working year, but who may not be cast in any of them, how is that 'free work' justified? It can't simply be the case that actors justify their preparation and attendance at auditions on the basis of how many parts they successfully get. I've been in this business long enough to have known actors who have auditioned for many years and still have had very little or even no success. So how are they justifying their time? How do they see their purpose, and how do they see the purpose of all those fruitless auditions? And in the case of actors who find out later that someone absurd got the part ('I can't believe they cast him/her!') – surely that is the actor's equivalent of watching their Bionicle being taken apart before their eyes?

Going with the flow

We probably don't spend much time thinking about doing unpaid work-related activities, even though everyone who auditions is working for free. Dedicating yourself to hard practice, in order that you might achieve mastery in something that you can't be certain will pay off, is a *risk*. But it's a risk that every serious performer has to take. The question is: How much hard work should you be putting into your performing skills 'on spec'? We've looked at the kind of hours it takes to achieve mastery in the last chapter, and we have to admit that committing ourselves to this kind of practice and effort is a huge decision to take. But before you can decide how much work you would agree to take on in this speculative way you have to have a genuine sense of what, in your life, you consider work and what you consider leisure, and when it comes to some activities that is a tough question to answer.

For performers, artists, athletes and many other professional pursuits, we have to admit that the activities involved in this kind of work can be difficult to place in the category of 'work' or 'leisure'. I remember seeing comedian Chris Rock do a terrific monologue[8] on the difference between having a job and having a career. For Rock, the difference really comes down to time. When you have a career there's never enough time for you get around to all the things you want to do. When you have a job, there's far too much time, and Rock's 'job' character is amazed at how slowly time goes by when he's doing mindless tasks in a kitchen restaurant. Rock's observation has interesting correlations with Mikhail Csikszentmihalyi's carefully conceived idea of the 'flow' state, in which we pursue something in such a focused manner that time really has no meaning for us. In the 'flow' state we are 'completely involved in an activity for its own sake. The ego falls away. Time flies. Every action, movement, and thought follows inevitably from the previous one, like playing jazz. Your whole being is involved, and you're using your skills to the utmost.'[9] While most of us would recognise this description, we also know how hard it is to get into that flow state in any sustained way. We also know it's unlikely that we'll get into it unless we're finding it for ourselves. As one of the people involved in the work study of commissioned/non-commissioned artists we looked at earlier explained:

> Not always, but a lot of the time, when you are doing a piece for someone else it becomes more 'work' than joy. When I work for myself there is the pure joy of creating and I can work through the night and not even know it. On a commissioned piece you have to check yourself – be careful to do what the client wants.[10]

This probably sounds familiar, especially the last part about wanting to please a client (in our case an audition panel). You probably recognise instinctively that you'd be a better performer if you could get into that state of the 'pure joy of creating'. At many points in your rehearsal and work you may have felt yourself to be in that state, and if you can remember what kinds of activities you were doing at the time then you're some way toward figuring out what the difference between a work and a leisure activity is for you.

However, even if we can answer that question – and can determine what it is about our own performing work that gets us into the state of 'flow' – could we ever aspire to be in that state when we're in front of an audition panel? We might very well get there when we're performing, but doesn't the whole nerve-wracking experience of auditioning bring up too many worries about 'pleasing the client' to allow us to perform for them in full 'flow'? Maybe this question can only ever be answered in the affirmative if we can get ourselves into the state where auditioning doesn't feel like work, but instead feels like pleasure.

> There's a thing I've always loved about opera singers when they audition or perform. All those years of practice makes them really want to show you what they can do. They walk into a room and you can just see the joy of performing for them – they've spent so much time practising, they just can't wait to perform. It's infectious.
>
> Trevor Jackson

It's clear that deciding what feels like work and what just feels like a joy is a very personal act. For me, mathematics in any form, calculator or not, is hard work and gives me horrors whenever I have to do it. But I know mathematicians who swear that it's more exciting than I can possibly imagine, akin to any other kind of creative problem solving, and brings all the same kinds of challenge and exhilaration if only you know the language. That's probably true. But in the meantime, for me, maths is hard work. I could never get into that 'flow' state with it because my skill level is too low to attain any measure of satisfaction in doing it. But I can reach that state easily when I'm singing, and you probably do as well when you're performing and your imagination is fully engaged in what you're doing. This state is evidently where we would all *like* to be when we're auditioning, but how do we get there and how, exactly, do we define 'flow'?

Csikszentmihalyi has developed a structured approach to the ways in which we might conceive of the flow state and the optimal experience. He suggests that it all comes down to a ratio between skill level and level of challenge. For him, the flow state starts when both the skill level and the level of challenge are high. If the challenge is too high for the level of skill we'll simply be frustrated or anxious. If the challenge is too low for the level of skill we won't be engaged. But when challenge level meets skill level in an activity that we enjoy, we can often find ourselves in that flow state and this is where the question of what motivates us becomes pretty critical. As we've seen, people who are motivated by a high fear of failure tend to choose tasks that are too easy or too difficult, while people who are motivated by achievement tend to match skills to challenges pretty well.

When we are working on a challenge that is a good match for our skill set, and when the challenge is based in something we love doing, then time seems unimportant: we're too focused on what we're doing to even think about it. So the question that naturally arises is: What kind of work results in the 'flow state' for you? Hopefully your answer is performing. If so, a second question arises: Can you rehearse for hours on end in a focused, happy, 'time-flies-by' way? This leads to a third question: Can you engineer your practice/rehearsal times so that you can be in that state as often as possible?

If you can answer 'Yes' to the last two questions you've taken the first great step to committing to the kind of time that it takes to create confidence and a sense of mastery, and while confidence and mastery might not be entirely sufficient for defining the 'it' factor of auditions, they are almost certainly necessary elements. If we know we need to rack up 10,000 hours of experience we can only conceive of achieving that if we are highly motivated and engaged in the pursuit itself.

One stone and the 'greater glory'

As we've seen, what really matters for us is intrinsic motivation, so we need to consider how that works. We know that when we think closely about our own intrinsic drive for doing things there are two ways in which we can characterise our motivation: we might be 'motivated toward' (achievement) or 'motivated away from' things (like failure). If what is driving us is a passion to be onstage in a leading role in the West End, then we're 'motivated toward' that goal. If what is driving us is a general fear of failure, or a passion to get away from a dead-end job, then we're 'motivated away from' something. In other words, our focus isn't so much about attaining a goal. Instead, our focus is to avoid something. For many reasons, research suggests that we will perform better if we're motivated toward a goal and not away from a given situation. Performance coach Jeremy Lazarus explains this a little more clearly:

> How can 'away from' motivation cause sub-optimal results? There are two main ways. Firstly ... what we focus on increases. So if the reason you want something is because you want to avoid the negative consequences of not having it, you'll be thinking about not having, which paradoxically makes it more likely that you won't have it!
>
> Secondly, if a sports person's primarily 'away from' motivated, once they have moved away from what they don't want, they can lose interest and motivation.[11]

Lazarus sees this as the explanation for things like 'yo-yo' dieting: those cases where the dieter thinks 'I don't want to be overweight' and then loses the motivation to eat in a healthy way as soon as they do lose weight. Of course, if the dieter starts out thinking 'I want to be fit, healthy and the right weight', it is far more likely that they will be focusing on the right positive outcome, and motivation is likely to remain robust as long as the commitment is powerful enough in the first place. All of this leads us back to the question of whether our commitment is powerful enough (which surely depends on what's motivating us) and should make us realise that this is both a tough and a critical question when it comes to auditioning. We can't make a 'yo-yo' commitment to being great performers – we have to make a long-term commitment if we're serious.

In the case of performers I often run into people who are driven by the desire to prove someone wrong (a high school teacher, their father, etc.). This is a version of being 'motivated away from': in this case 'motivated away from' parental disapproval or a teacher's critical eye. As we've seen, these kind of motivations can be very strong in the first instance, but the problem for a performer in the 'motivated away from' situation is that once they attain approval they may find that they have no further motivation. Because the visualised goal is important in goal setting and keeping your focus (and let's face it, if you need to be logging up the hours, you'll need to be doing both of those things), you'll maintain your motivation better if you're working toward something positive.

So could we imagine our lives working in such a way that purpose, motivation and activity were all aligned? Could we imagine dedicating ourselves to our art by putting in many hours of practice and concentrating closely on building up our mental stamina and monitoring our thoughts and language so that they continually support, rather than sabotage, our efforts? Is this a state that we can actually achieve? By now it should be clear that this is what demonstrating confidence and mastery as we walk into the audition room requires. But perhaps we still need to answer the questions raised at the beginning of this chapter: What is our purpose in auditioning and why would we be doing all this in the first place?

Let's go back to consider the two common answers to this question in audition interviews. At this point we can recognise that 'I can't see myself doing anything else' is a 'motivated away from' answer, while the second 'I've always loved performing' answer is at least a positive, 'motivated toward' statement. Answers such as 'It's what I've always wanted to do' also puts the case positively, but as often as not I – like many panel members who witness one poor audition after another – wonder whether these people really do love performing. Surely a love of performing would result in better performance? We probably secretly conclude that what the person we've just seen really loves is attention, and that is a troublesome love to bring into a casting room. I know no end of casting agents, directors and acting teachers who moan about the simple-minded motivation of *fame*. There are many people in the industry that will happily spend hours telling you about the horrors wrought by reality television and its lamentable by-product: the get-famous-for-nothing mentality.

There's little to be said for or about this: anyone who wants fame for its own sake is probably deluded about the decidedly mixed joys of being famous. And who knows whether the idealised notion of attaining fame is actually strong enough to motivate people for hours on end? If it is, then perhaps it is as good a motivational driver as anything else. But we have to remember that it would only drive someone to fame, and not to excellence, so it's important to be clear about what you're after. I think that knowing why you want to work in the performing arts and what your objectives are should be at the heart of everything performers do.

An old story tells of a visitor who encounters three stone-masons working on a medieval cathedral, and asks each what he is doing. 'I am cutting this stone to shape,' says the first, describing his basic actions. 'I am building a great cathedral,' says the second, describing his immediate goal. 'And I am working for the glory of God,' says the third, describing his high-level objective.[12]

This story is retold by John Kay in his book *Obliquity*, as he considers the relevance of having immediate goals, intermediate goals, and 'high-level' objectives. As I read it I wondered whether I had ever been, or if I had ever met, the kind of auditioning performer who could identify all three objectives. I don't think I have, but I'm convinced that this kind of thinking would help us to make sense of so many things in our lives, not simply success or lack of it in auditioning.

If we *could* identify what's driving us – now, in the short-term future and in the longer term – wouldn't we be much more capable of adopting a mental 'relaxedness' about the audition we have tomorrow? If a given audition is making us nervous enough to demonstrate all the physical sensations of panic – racing heart, sweaty palms, dry mouth – or to go 'blank' when it comes to remembering lines, etc., surely that level of panic would be reduced if, like the stone-masons above, we could learn to see this one audition as simply a 'stone' that we're cutting. That single stone is, of course, important in the construction of the cathedral, but it isn't, in itself, going to make a massive difference to the larger goal of celebrating a 'greater glory'.

Seen in this way, a high-level objective may be just the thing for helping us to keep individual audition experiences in perspective and to help keep the 'metaphorical weight' of that audition down to a manageable level.

Perhaps Csikszentmihalyi puts it best:

> In the lives of many people it is possible to find a unifying purpose that justifies the things they do day in, day out – a goal that like a magnetic field attracts their psychic energy, a goal upon which all lesser goals depend. This goal will define the challenges that a person needs to face in order to transform his or her life into a flow activity. Without such a purpose, even the best-ordered consciousness lacks meaning.[13]

Surely we can only benefit by giving the random, maddening audition experiences of our lives some meaning?

Summary

In this section we have considered a great number of things that affect us in our auditions: some of which are in our control and some of which are not. Having looked closely at the whole process, and hopefully in a new way, we're ready to take on the practical work of building a real strategy for mastering the audition experience. We'll be considering how we deal with our fears, how we ensure that we're setting and attaining positive goals, and how we learn to avoid some of the worst of the 'side-effects' of auditioning (particularly in terms of adding a lot of 'metaphorical weight'). We'll also make a training plan both for developing skills and technique and for developing a kind of mental toughness that can see us through the whole process. As this chapter has revealed, motivation is key and we'll be spending some time in trying to ensure that we have practical ways of understanding just what it is that motivates us and also that we have some solid plans for harnessing and exploiting that motivation as we work toward perfecting our audition 'game'.

PART 2:
THE TOOLKIT

7 KNOWING WHERE YOU'RE GOING

When creativity has become your habit; when you've learned to manage time, resources, expectations, and the demands of others; when you understand the value and place of validation, continuity, and purity of purpose – then you're on the way to an artist's ultimate goal: the achievement of mastery.[1]

Twyla Tharp

This section of the book is all about putting the ideas of the first half into a practical plan for yourself that can help you to get your skills, your artistry and your mental game on track for improved audition performance. The exercises included are designed to help you get focused, stay motivated and create a strategy for your career development.

The exercises will require some soul-searching and a bit of dedication, but they will change some of the ways in which you currently work, and much of the way that you currently think of yourself in terms of audition.

The curse of the 'self-help' book

These days if you take a look at any large bookstore's holdings in the 'popular psychology' or 'self-help' sections you will see everything from how to organise your time, to how to be happy, to how to get what you want by ordering things through the 'cosmos'. Many of these books have attracted a lot of criticism and it's easy to understand why. There's an undeniable aura of simplicity about them, and I'm often amazed at the simple ways in which they imagine the complexity of the human psyche. But there are some ideas that emerge regularly in self-help books that also emerge in serious business books and sports-psychology books as well. And there is both strong research and general agreement about the fact that these ideas can have a powerful effect on our behaviour.

One of these ideas is goal setting and having an overall strategy for getting from where you are now to where you want to be. Businesses don't run without a strategic plan and coaches don't take on athletes without working out a training plan. Strategic and training plans both have very clearly defined goals, partly because of the power language has in terms of how we view our ability to control our immediate environment (and the ways in which we interpret that environment), and partly because having clearly defined ideas about what we want to do, why we're doing it and what we hope will result from doing it keeps us focused on getting to where we want to go. This is just common sense, but there has also been much research looking into the relationship between goal setting and performance, and without doubt all that research suggests that we simply *perform better* when we set goals. Indeed, it appears that the harder the goal, the better the performance:

> Hard goals result in a higher level of performance than do easy goals, and specific hard goals result in a higher level of perform- ance than do no goals or a generalised 'do your best'.[2]

According to Edwin Locke and Gary Latham (research psychologists who have devoted their lives to the study of goal setting), this may be because the act of setting goals does four very specific things for us – they:

1. Direct our attention
2. Energise us
3. Boost our persistence
4. Inspire us to draw on existing knowledge and also to create new strategies and approaches to problem solving.[3]

There are also some very interesting ideas that accompany this kind of research, which are related to what really matters when we set goals.

For example, it has been proven many times that the goals we tend to achieve most often are the ones we set ourselves. It's also been shown that those with higher self-esteem have a greater chance of reaching their goals than those with low self-esteem. It has also more recently been shown that people tend to work harder to reach goals if they think that in achieving them they are doing something good, boosting self-esteem and therefore increasing their chances of achieving their goals.

However, as we've seen, the whole area of goal setting is a complicated one, because how we set them and whether we stick to them can raise a lot of questions about what inspired our desires in the first place, and whether sticking to them doggedly in the face of changing circumstances is a good idea or not. Still, we're going be working out a plan here, and that plan depends on being able to set goals in a smart, positive way. So we'll be taking this one step at a time and before we even think about creating a little strategy for audition (and therefore career) success, we have to have some idea of where we are now. In other words, we can't begin to map out a future without knowing where we're starting from.

What is it you REALLY want?

> So, what is the secret of a good audition then? Talent, many might say, and while right in some respects, it is not what I would answer. Being right for the part is another strong contender, and plays a large part in my answer, which is . . . confidence. Easier said than done, I hear you cry, but there are tricks to boost confidence. [4]

Actors are a bit like dieters. Being both a dieter and an actor, I know that we are always on the lookout for shortcuts that work and I know it's very frustrating to find out that they don't exist. The quote above, from Richard Evans, suggests that there are some short-term 'tricks' that help to boost confidence and I'm sure his ideas could be helpful in a pinch. But what we're talking about here isn't short-term anything. We're talking about the biggest decision you'll ever make in your life (your career and its progress), and that means that if we want to succeed over the long term we have to recognise what success in this very tough industry is going to take. My view on this has been emphasised enough in the first section: it's going to take mastery. It's going take the kind of absolute confidence that isn't built on shortcuts or blagging, but on a solid knowledge of the industry, of your own abilities and skills, of the context and practice of what you do and on the careful and dedicated honing of your work as an expressive artist. This is why training is so important.

> I think our actors, particularly in the younger generation, are not really getting the training they need. I think it's the reason why we tend to look in England and Australia. And actors here in America wonder why we do so much casting from there. It's because most of them have had some professional training.
>
> I will say to a young actor: what actors do you admire? Because, most likely, those actors have had some training. They all took classes for years and I do think that trained actors have so much more to draw on. Having just cast *Hugo* – look at the actors who are in the film. They are all theatre actors; they are all trained actors.
>
> *Ellen Lewis*

Mastering your art requires a lot, but most certainly it requires two things: passion and dedication. So the first point in this journey is to examine carefully what it is we truly want. Because without knowing that, we'll never marshall the motivation we need to see us through this great project. Why is this so important? Well, I might think that I want to be a world-class piano player. But the thought of putting in all those hours of practice doing scales, arpeggios and working repeatedly on my technique as well as my artistry just does not appeal to me. I know that I simply wouldn't have the discipline to do it. And the reason I don't have that kind of discipline is because, in truth, I'm not passionate enough about playing the piano to dedicate my life in that way. The only logical conclusion I can come to about this is that I probably don't really want to be a concert pianist – I probably just like the idea of the standing ovations and the nice concert halls. Or I might also fantasise about being a 100-metre hurdler. But the simple act of thinking about putting in six hours a day on the track and in the gym is a very quick way of making me realise that I don't *really* want to be a 100-metre hurdler – I just want the gold medal. So how is it different for performers?

My argument, of course, is that it isn't. If the thought of putting in ten to twelve hours a week gives you the shakes, or sounds impossible or uninteresting to you, then I would suggest that maybe performing isn't your passion at all. Maybe you just want an Oscar. That's fine – who wouldn't want an Oscar? But this is the point at which you have to be honest. You would laugh at me if I said that I wanted to be a leading ballerina in the Royal Ballet but I didn't want to spend hours in a dance studio perfecting my technique and my expressivity. Or that I wanted to be invited to the European Athletics Championships, but I didn't want to go to the gym or run time trials. For both the dancer and the elite athlete there's more than just the 'end game' to consider. Of course the competition is important, and of course they want the gold medal or the standing ovation. But just as important is the way in which they are driven to better themselves, to set themselves goals and to compete with their own 'personal best' achievements. And for both dancer and athlete, the drive to be the very best that they can is a strong inner motivation that makes all the hours and the pain worthwhile.

This kind of motivation needs to be something from deep within: something that drives you with a fury that keeps you going no matter how hard the work. This is called 'intrinsic motivation' and we'll look more closely at this idea later. But what I'm suggesting here is that if the idea of practising ten to twelve hours a week doesn't appeal to you, then becoming a great performer (and mastering the process of both performing and auditioning) is probably not a reasonable goal for you. Additionally, you have to know whether you're ready to take on something that demanding. How can you tell?

EXERCISE ONE

Take a moment and answer the following questions as honestly as you can:

1. *When I'm working on a monologue or song, or rehearsing, I get lost in the process and almost feel like time 'stands still':* **YES/NO**
2. *When I look at my work critically (and think about how people have responded to my work in the past) I know where my strengths and my weaknesses lie:* **YES/NO**
3. *If I had the time, I know exactly what I'd like to be working on:* **YES/NO**
4. *When I have free time I often spend it reading, going to a gallery or seeing performances of some kind:* **YES/NO**
5. *When I watch other actors I feel like I can articulate my views on what makes their acting either good or bad:* **YES/NO**
6. *I would find it easy to design a serious plan of work for myself in terms of my technique:* **YES/NO**

If you answered at least four of these questions with a 'Yes', you're probably ready to start taking your career seriously, and here's why.

1. *When I'm working on a monologue or song, or rehearsing, I get lost in the process and almost feel like time 'stands still'.* If you can answer 'Yes' to this question, you're at the point where you easily achieve 'flow': a state that has been written about and discussed intensively.[5] This is the point where challenges are just slightly ahead of your current skill. It means that you aren't frustrated by the difficulty of the challenge you set, but instead are focused on meeting it. If a challenge is too great for your skillset you'll simply be frustrated. If it's too simple for your abilities, you'll be bored. The goal for successful training is to keep challenges at the right level so that you can easily find yourself slipping into that 'flow' state.
2. *When I look at my work critically (and think about how people have responded to my work in the past) I know where my*

strengths and my weaknesses lie. If you can do this, you're able to design a programme of work for yourself. If you have a good idea what kind of vocal, physical and imaginative challenges you need to set for yourself, then you should also have some sense of being able to judge whether you are becoming more flexible and strong in the areas you perceive as weaknesses. Of course, it's always a good idea to have some outside coaching or at the very least a rehearsal partner that you can discuss this with (we'll talk about finding a 'team' to support your efforts in Chapter 8).

3. *If I had the time, I know exactly what I'd like to be working on.* If you are thinking in this way then you're part-way toward putting your plan into action. If you already know what you'd like to work on, your challenge is one of carving out the space to embark on the work and, in a sense, that makes things a lot easier. Of course, time is always a challenge, but you would have that challenge anyway. If you're savvy enough to know what you should be working on, you will be that much more focused on facing the challenge of clearing time in your life to get to it.

4. *When I have free time I read, go to a gallery or go to see performing artists.* Of course, no one spends *all* their leisure time in these areas, but if you're able to say that you do spend a good proportion of your time engaging with the work of other actors, visual or performing artists, and writers, then you are probably already better educated than many performers and better able to articulate what it is that makes a particular piece of art interesting, or what makes a particular actor's work so exciting. If you are truly fascinated by human expression you will be well ahead of many other auditioning performers, not only because your general knowledge of the arts will be greater, but because, for you, it is likely that your ability to link your own particular goals to a higher motivation will be stronger.

5. *When I watch other actors I feel like I can articulate my views on what makes their acting either good or bad.* Being passionate in

your views about what makes great acting or great performance is a big part of what gives you the stamina and the vision to work and to discipline yourself. It doesn't mean that your views have to accord with those of others – it simply means that you have to have a view about what makes great work. That view emerges out of many years of watching, learning and debating about performances and finding that the more you engage in discussion, the better you are able to articulate for yourself regarding what makes a great performance. If you're already able to say 'Yes' to this question, you're on the way to knowing what it is you want to get from your own work as an interpretive artist.

6. *I would find it easy to design a serious plan of work for myself in terms of technique.* If you can't imagine what you could possibly do for an hour or two a day in practice, then you probably don't know enough about how performers train, or about what you actually need to do to improve your own work. It's likely that you haven't spent enough time in classes or reading to be able to work independently. But if you think you are able to do this, then you're probably ready to get on with it right now.

If you could only answer a few of these questions with a 'Yes', you probably need more input in terms of training, practice and reading. Often, even performers who have had a full three years' training in a conservatoire can feel a bit uncertain about how they would go about designing their own programme of continual growth and enhancement, and that is probably as much to do with the rather institutionalised and controlled system of teaching in conservatoires as it does with a training student's sense of 'powerlessness'. We rely too much on directors, teachers and coaches at times and that can sometimes leave us with the feeling that answering the questions above is beyond us. But being able to answer these questions positively is the first step toward being able to audition with confidence.

If you feel at this point that the idea of designing your own programme of work and dedicating yourself to spending at least ten hours a week on your performing technique is just too much to contemplate, then no doubt it's time to have a serious rethink about what you're doing and what you truly want to do. If performing is something that you truly want to do then the idea of really dedicating yourself will be an exciting one. But if you're just in it for the Oscar . . . well, good luck. Because luck is what you'll have to rely on.

Still thinking about that Oscar

Assuming you haven't closed this book and applied to do a degree in business administration you are probably thinking about how to incorporate between ten and twelve hours of practice into your week, what that might feel like, and how you would keep yourself motivated. We don't tend to think of working by ourselves, and we don't tend to think about rehearsing without others around. That is because we're used to working in ways that rely on others to make judgements for us. So the very first thing we will need to do is to rethink how it is that violinists and long-jumpers work for hours on end on their own. The answer to that is simple enough: they have tangible goals and they work toward them. Performing artists, of course, don't have a seventeen-foot mark they're trying to hit, so one of our first tasks will be to design the kinds of goals that will help us to set 'markers' of our achievement.

Some are simple enough. We might decide that we know what difference half an hour of vocal work a day will do for us, so we could easily set this as a target and make sure that, at certain points, we're recording ourselves or having other experienced people listen and comment on any progress that they hear. However, in that vocal work it is important to know exactly what our goals are for the voice. We might also decide that twenty to thirty minutes of physical work every day will make a significant difference in our performance and confidence and, again, we could set that as part of a working target.

But what about the more artistic (and less tangible) goals of interpretation, expression and characterisation, or of making powerful and risky acting choices? Can we set about creating a kind of practice that can be tested in these areas? Perhaps the question isn't really framed properly; because setting a 'goal' for a performance is an idea that strikes us intuitively as impossible. We couldn't imagine a 'goal' as we work on Hamlet, for example, apart from becoming more confident about how we interpret and express the role, and surely that just comes from having spent a lot of time working on Hamlet?

Before we launch into the practicalities of working in a dedicated way, there are some important things that we need to consider. We need to do a little soul searching about what we value in life, about how our performing and auditioning is related to that, and about how we can know that this is really what we want. In other words, before we start to create a strategy for success, we need to take a step back and look at why we've chosen performing arts as a career in the first place.

How can we be sure that we've launched ourselves into the right life choice and that we aren't choosing an impossible dream here because it cushions the fear of failure? As we've seen, there is some serious research that suggests choosing impossible dreams can be a way of easing the blow of failure (i.e., comforting yourself with the knowledge that it's such a competitive business it would be exceptional if you *don't* fail). How can we ensure that we're not pursuing a 'destructive goal' path? Well, we're in very difficult territory here, and I'm profoundly aware that very little has been written about this area and that there is relatively little research to base any judgement on.

Learning from Mt Everest

There have been many times, when watching an audition performance, when I've felt absolutely certain that the person I'm watching has chosen the wrong profession. It's hard to watch people making the wrong choices, and I can't tell you how many times I've wondered about the ethics of some training courses that have taken on students who clearly won't ever reach the kind of standard demanded by the industry. Often, when I'm watching these people and hearing their declarations of dedication to the profession, I can't help wondering if the pursuit of their goal to be a famous actor isn't the perfect example of 'destructive goal' pursuit. Of course, reality therapy tends to sort many of these people out fairly quickly. But assuming you have actually chosen a career that you have a chance at, and before you can really proceed to designing a strategy for upping your audition game, you still need to be sure that what you're pursuing here isn't actually a set of destructive goals. This means that no matter what your current or potential talents and abilities may be, you have to be certain that you're not pursuing a narrow outcome in a doggedly stubborn way. How can you tell?

EXERCISE TWO

Take a moment to answer this question:

Why have you chosen performing as your career path, and why do you stay with it?

Don't answer too quickly – really take some time to consider it. When did the idea first occur to you? How long have you wanted to do this? Why has it taken up such an important place in your life? You might also begin this contemplation by thinking about the whole of your journey – from your very first performance up until now. Put this book down and just meditate on that question for half an hour or so. Give yourself time to really think about this, and then write what comes to you:

I chose performing arts as a career because:

WATFORD LRC

I stay with it because:

```



```

Now that you've written this, have a look at how it's stated. Is it stated in the 'motivated toward' way? Or is it stated in the 'motivated away from' area? If it's all about being motivated toward something, that's fine. If it's all about being a performer because you don't want to be an accountant like your dad, or about staying with it because you'll look like a failure if you give up, go back and try to write it out again in positive, 'motivated toward' language.

Once you've done this, go back to the warning signs listed in Kayes' book (below). You might want to consider whether or not you find some resonance between his list, your own answers above, and the way in which you think you generally approach the whole business of being an auditioning performer:

1. *Narrowly defined goals*: as we know, 'It's all I've ever seen myself doing' is a recurring theme in audition interviews, and for performers who are starting out, staying focused is important. You won't climb Everest successfully if you start by thinking that you'll go a little way and then see how you feel. You'll only get there if the summit is your goal from the start. But if conditions change, or become adverse, then you have to be flexible if you want to stay alive. How can you/should you hold on to this goal if you're never auditioning successfully?

2. *Weight of public expectation*: I know many performers for whom the idea of telling their friends that they might give it up would feel embarrassing or shameful. But surely the only advantage to pursuing such a highly competitive career is that there should never be any shame in changing your direction?

No one starts out worrying about this, but some performers find that, as they go along, the expectation of others becomes a worrying factor in their decision to stay with it.

3. *Face-saving behaviour*: I will not be the only person who knows someone who insists that they are an actor after waiting tables for ten years. This isn't necessarily an issue, but it is one of a number of behaviours that might be destructive for us if we are also exhibiting many of the other warning signs.

4. *Idealised future*: probably the saddest phone call I ever get is not from the ex-student who *hasn't* been successful, but from the ex-student who *has*. It's common to think that if we get work once – especially high-profile work – we'll always have work. But the fact is that I've known some incredibly successful people who've gone through some bleak periods without work. That is the reality of this business, and there are very few exceptions. Some people can't get cast simply because their first role was too well-known or too successful. Some people can't get cast simply because they seem only to fit a narrow range of roles, and these might not come up with regularity. Some *can* get cast and then find out very quickly just how mind-numbing eight shows a week in the West End can be. There are many ways in which this profession is idealised by people who aren't in it. It may be that what inspired you was the 'ideal', but will this be enough once you're facing the realities of the business? Do your research and make sure you have a good idea of what success in this business means.

5. *Goal-driven justification*: this is the 'I've said I'm going to be an actor and I can't stop until I am' syndrome. It's associated with warning sign number two above and is related to feeling that once we've headed in a given direction, it will be shameful or wrong to change.

6. *Associating a goal with 'destiny'*: this is hard to refute, and many times I've heard people tell an audition panel that they've always just 'known' that performing is what they're meant to do in this life. The problem is that so many people

who really *are* successful often say much the same thing in interviews. While this kind of certainty may be incredibly helpful (and we'll look at the importance of 'irrational optimism' later), we also need to remember that there is a very thin line between goal-oriented focus and self-delusion, which proves just how complex human behaviour can be – and how careful we have to be when trying to set and monitor our own future goals.[6]

If you recognise yourself here, don't despair. We're just at the beginning of our process and the most important thing is that you are honest with yourself. I hope the exercises that follow will be helpful, because they're designed to ensure that you don't fall into any of these traps as you progress and also to keep your goal-setting ideas both flexible and broad. Getting where you want to go means setting goals and pursuing them, but it also means keeping them broad and recognising all the alternative, positive outcomes that a given range of goals can produce. Once we identify and recognise all those possible outcomes, we can avoid setting destructive goals.

Setting meaningful goals always involves thinking hard about what matters to us, and how we approach what we do – not just as actors, but in general. The following exercises are designed to help focus your mind on some fundamental values and visions. You might just want to jump right in, or you might find it helpful to start by reading through the sample answers first, which start on page 109, and then fill in the blank worksheets below for yourself. These exercises will take a few hours to complete, so make sure you start when you've got some quiet, uninterrupted time to yourself. For the last exercise you'll also need a journal or a notebook that you can keep referring to as we proceed through the whole second section of this book.

EXERCISE THREE

Try to find some quiet, concentrated time for this exercise if you can, and suspend judgement for a moment as you go through. Every coach in the world – whether they're from the world of business or sport – will tell you that until you know what you value, you can't entirely figure out how to motivate yourself.

If you had to imagine yourself at the end of your life, what are the three things that you most hope will be remembered about you?

```
1.

2.

3.
```

Imagine you've just won the lottery. It's a big one – you'll never have to work again. Of course, you buy property for yourself and your family and you go on some fabulously restful long vacations. But once that initial rush is over, you decide you must make a list of priorities. What are the top three things you want to do?

```
1.
2.
3.
```

Imagine that you won that Oscar tomorrow and that in your acceptance speech you can only thank four people or entities. Who/what would they be?

```
1.

2.

3.

4.
```

Now that you've listed your four people or entities, try to think of what each of them might name as the one thing they value most in life.

```
1.

2.

3.

4.
```

Keeping in mind all of the answers above (which should just help to prepare your thinking for this), put the following things in order from your point of view:

Family	Charity
Success	Security
Money	Tranquillity
Relationships with friends	Intelligence
Relationship with partner	Excitement
God/Buddha/Mohammed/	Health
the creator or any kind of	Wisdom
religious entity	Integrity
Goodness/kindness	Power
Creativity	

The point of this exercise is to figure out what really matters to you. That is never easy to do, and sometimes it's interesting to note what kinds of values we have accepted from others, and what things we have come to value in our own right. This final list – while it may be influenced by all the preceding questions – should represent what you really value in your life. Getting to grips with that is the key to staying motivated.

List your top five values here:

1.

2.

3.

4.

5.

EXERCISE FOUR

Using your answers above, we're going to link these values to the idea of why you're going to be working so hard to master your art. This is a slightly different type of exercise, and it requires that you imagine yourself writing your Oscar acceptance speech. One of the things you decide to do in this speech is create a personal statement that explains what has really driven your success.

Take your time with this because it's going to be the basis of your working plan. <u>Make sure you refer to your 'top 5 values' list above</u>. You could start your sentence with any of the following:

My success as an actor is based on my belief in . . .
My success as an actor allows me to . . .
My success as an actor is completely down to . . .
My success as an actor will . . .

This isn't just about making yourself a better person by 'living your values' – the fact is that research has shown that linking your life goals to your values makes a significant difference in your ability to reach those goals. As Daniel Pink points out: 'People working toward mastery perform at very high levels. But those who do so in the service of some greater objective can achieve even more. The most deeply motivated people – not to mention those who are most productive

and satisfied – hitch their desires to a cause larger than themselves.'[7]
As you write out your Oscar acceptance speech it should help you to
clarify which things really are important to your work and your creative process.

So many possible futures

We know that life often takes us in directions that we never planned
for. But if unpredictability is frustrating, it can often be exciting as
well. It may seem odd to think about planning for alternative futures
when we're busy planning our acting career, but if many years in this
business have taught me nothing else, they've taught me that there is
wisdom in considering the 'unconsiderable'. In this next exercise we're
going to spend a little time imagining at least one other possible
future for ourselves. This isn't only about helping to keep our goal-
setting positively broad, but also to help us keep our perspective when
we're in the middle of thinking that we must 'perform or die'. Perhaps
a quick tale will help inspire you.

   One of my classmates at University regularly pops up on Facebook,
and his life has moved in a very different direction to that which it
was heading when we were in graduate school together. I love to see
the photos he posts of his vineyard in Oregon and I think he's one of
the happiest of the graduates of our particular time. I knew that he
had grown up in an agricultural setting, but when we were studying
together he never mentioned going back home or getting back into
farming – he just wanted to be an actor. So I've been pleasantly
surprised by his success as a winemaker and asked him a bit about his
journey. He thinks that the wine industry is a lot like the theatre
community: growers share ideas in very open ways and he is proud of
the fact that he currently supplies grapes to other wine makers and
stays involved in a larger community of growers. He hasn't given up
on acting entirely and thinks that he will work again as an actor in the
future. But for now wine-making is his passion, and when I see his
posts on Facebook it's not hard to imagine why. He isn't the only actor
I've known to happily change directions, but he is the only one whose

vineyard pictures regularly make me fantasise about another kind of life.

EXERCISE FIVE

Non-destructive, positive goal setting is the aim here, and as we go through we'll be looking at how to list goals that aren't fatally narrow. One way to avoid narrow goal setting, is to make sure that every goal has multiple outcomes and that every goal includes strategic alternatives that can accommodate changing circumstances. If you need a little guidance in responding to this exercise, try reading the sample answers first (starting on page 109).

Primary career vision:
Start by imagining exactly what you envision will be happening in your performing career five years from today:
Bearing in mind where you imagine you will be in five years' time, list five

positive side-effects of your achievements. These should be things that are not directly related to what you're doing (performing) but that have come about as a result of your success:
List two things that your success has done for others:

1.
2.
3.
4.
5.

Alternative career vision:

1.

2.

Now, as a purely imaginative exercise, describe an alternative vision of your life five years from today. This can be any alternative life you can imagine for yourself, as long as the idea of living it is one that you think will make you happy:
Looking at your five positive side-effects listed above, imagine how they

---

---

might relate to your alternative future vision:

1.

2.

3.

4.

5.

Finally, complete this sentence with five alternative endings: Whatever form my future life takes, mastering performance will enhance . . .

1.

2.

3.

4.

5.

The point of the 'alternative' part of the exercise is *not* to derail your dreams of performing. It is simply to help you keep in mind the wider good that could come from all the effort you put into mastering your art. It should also result in demonstrating very clearly why – no matter what decisions an audition panel may come to in your case – your work in mastering your craft is never wasted, and is always contributing to your greater good and overall improvement. That knowledge – as we've seen in the case of the Bionicle builders – can, in itself, help to keep you motivated.

Sample Answers: Exercises Three to Five

Below are sample answers to Exercises Three, Four and Five above, which were supplied by my volunteer army of actors. They're here just to help you get a sense of how to work through the questions above.

Exercise Three
If you had to imagine yourself at the end of your life, what are the three things that you most hope will be remembered about you?

1. *That I was kind and generous*

2. *That I lived an 'examined' life and was intellectually curious*

3. *That I was creative*

Imagine you've just won the lottery. It's a big one – you'll never have to work again. Of course, you buy property for yourself and your family and you go on some fabulously restful long vacations. But once that initial rush is over, you decide you must make a list of priorities. What are the top three things you want to do?

> 1. *Start my own theatre company*
> 2. *Write a novel*
> 3. *Work for my favourite charity (Médicins Sans Frontières)*

Imagine that you won that Oscar tomorrow and that in your acceptance speech you can only thank four people or entities. Who/what would they be?

> 1. *My mother*
> 2. *My father*
> 3. *My 'creator' (I see this as a kind of universal energy)*
> 4. *My partner*

Now that you've listed your four people or entities, try to think of what each of them might name as the one thing they value most in life.

> 1. *Intelligence*
> 2. *Creativity*
> 3. *Being open to the process of life and staying positive whatever happens*
> 4. *Love*

Keeping in mind all of the answers above (which should just help to prepare your thinking for this), put the following things in order from your point of view

Family (1)	Relationships with friends
Goodness/kindness (2)	Money
Creativity (3)	God/Buddha/Mohammed/the creator
Relationship with partner (4)	or any kind of religious entity
Integrity (5)	Charity
Health	Tranquillity
Wisdom	Intelligence
Security	Excitement
Success	Power

List your top five values here:

1. *Family*
2. *Goodness/kindness*
3. *Creativity*
4. *Relationship with partner*
5. *Integrity*

Exercise Four
This volunteer's values were: (1) family; (2) integrity; (3) wisdom; (4) goodness/kindness; (5) creativity:

My success as an actor is completely down to the support I've been given by my family and by the ways in which our family has always valued individuality, integrity and creativity. I've learned over the years that what underlies a lot of my explorations when acting are exactly the things that underlie my relationship with my family: in our ups and downs, and in our tensions and our occasional serious traumas, we've all come to a kind of shared wisdom about the importance of forgiveness, kindness, compassion and patience with each other. We're getting a bit wiser as we get older. We may drive each other mad sometimes, but I know we'll always be there – supporting each other eventually, even if we don't always approve of each other's choices.

Exercise Five

Primary career vision:

Start by imagining what you envision will be happening in your performing career five years from today:

> I am working regularly and am well known as a 'jobbing actor' – I get good parts in both stage plays and television. My partner and I are married and we have bought a house. I am busy enough to make a comfortable living and overall the future looks good. I have a great agent and I am in demand as an actor, but I also have some control over my time. I enjoy acting and I feel greatly fulfilled in my career.

Bearing in mind where you imagine you will be in five years' time, list five positive side-effects of your achievements. These should be things that are not directly related to what you're doing (performing) but that have come about as a result of your success:

1. I am very confident in new situations and adapt quickly to different working conditions

2. My home life gives me stability

3. I am good at finding my own working opportunities and learned long ago not to rely on anyone else (agent!) solely for finding working opportunities

4. I have a powerful network of friends/people that I know and respect in the industry

5. I have really developed my critical faculties – I'm articulate about my own strengths and weaknesses and I'm confident about expressing my opinion on performance work

List two things that your success has done for others:

1. *I'm able to bring some joy into people's lives through performance*
2. *I have helped others trying to start in this business, by mentoring and teaching when I can*

Alternative career vision:

Now, as a purely imaginative exercise, describe an alternative vision of your life five years from today. This can be any alternative life you can imagine for yourself, as long as the idea of living it is one that you think will make you happy:

I have my own business, creating bespoke entertainment for corporate clients. I put together actors, singers, dancers, and musicians to provide high-quality, portable entertainment for premium business clients. My business is creative, fun, and very much in demand. My partner and I are married and we have bought a house. I make a comfortable living and I really enjoy what I do.

Looking at your five positive side-effects listed above, imagine how they might relate to your alternative future vision:

1. *Confidence/adaptable to new situations: every job is unique and requires that I be able to work confidently in a variety of venues and tailor the entertainment to a specific company*
2. *Stability: this contributes not only to my confidence but takes a lot of stress out of my life*
3. *Ability to find opportunities: I'm good at analysing market possibilities and finding work for my company*
4. *Networking: I've overcome my fear of networking, which helps in securing new bookings for my company*
5. *Enhanced critical ability: it's important that I know when something is quality or not, as corporate clients are very demanding*

Finally, complete this sentence with five alternative endings: Whatever form my future life takes, mastering performance will enhance . . .

1. My creativity
2. My empathy for others
3. My appreciation of the arts
4. My overall knowledge
5. My confidence

Finally

Go back now and look at your five values, then answer the following questions:

Do they make a good fit with both your Primary and Alternative career visions?

Do they match well with 'positive' side-effects?

The last bit of this chapter isn't about doing an exercise. It's about contemplation and writing. Having gone through all of this, you need to be able to see the practical worth of it. Much of that practical worth is connected to the metaphorical weight we want to lose around the whole business of auditioning. When we're in the midst of it all – the expectation, the nerves, the frustrated desires that make up auditions – things often take on greater significance than they should. Just knowing what we really want and what we really value in life can be a powerful weapon in reducing that exaggerated significance.

Knowing that all our hard work is continually making us better able to explore other opportunities and possibilities in life is important. Knowing that our hard work is never wasted is important. Feeling that what we're doing might benefit more than just ourselves is important and drives up our 'purpose motivation'. And making sure that we haven't narrowed our life goals in a way that invites disaster is critical. Keeping our goals flexible enough to cover alternative visions or futures means that we are able to take an oblique approach toward happiness, and surely that is what life is all about. We may all know that we want to be happy, and we may all think we know what that will take. But as John Kay points out, the difficulty in pursuing happiness is related to the difficulty in knowing what, exactly, will make us happy:

> Mountaineering is an extreme example of an apparently unpleasant activity undertaken by people who could be comfortable. But there are many others. Common leisure pursuits involve demanding physical effort. Men and women chase a ball around a field until they are too tired to stand. These routes to happiness are oblique. We make ourselves cold, wet and exhausted. We climb mountains only to descend again, we swim out to sea to be thrown back on land, we run until we are too tired to run any more. The determinants of happiness are evidently complicated.[8]

And so the determinants of how to audition happily are complicated. Even as we set goals and try to think carefully about what we want, we can only do so while simultaneously remembering just how complex the human psyche is and how hard it is to *know* just exactly what you want. Before you move on to the next chapter, spend some time writing in your journal. You aim should simply be to answer this question:

How does thinking about what really matters to me in my life help to put the business of auditions into perspective?

Summary

We've spent time in this section looking at our values, at how much we gain – in varying ways – from working hard on mastering our performance skills, at how we envision our future, and at how we can ensure that the goals we're setting in order to create that future are positive and wholly beneficial to us. It is really important that you have a sense that the work you put into your art pays off in ways that go beyond making you a better performer. It heightens your self-esteem, it broadens your knowledge and – as we've seen – it serves to prepare you for whatever the future may bring. This section forms the basis for all the other work we'll be doing in the next chapters of the toolkit, which are all about how to make our approach to auditioning and performing as confident and skilful as it can be. Our next step is to look at how we can create a strategy for developing our skills further.

8 DEVELOPING YOUR SKILL SET

A story to get us started

Once, many years ago in a remote place, a young man heard of a reclusive sword master who lived high in the hills. When people spoke of this master it was with reverence as he was undoubtedly the greatest and most skilled swordsman who had ever lived. The young man, whose greatest desire was to be a skilled warrior, decided to find the master. He travelled for many days up into the hills and finally found the old man meditating by a tree. Master, he said, I have travelled many days and found you in order to be your student. I wish to become a great warrior. The old man looked casually at him and replied that he would be happy to take him on as a student. His first task would be to cook dinner and clean up afterward. The young man took the task on happily. After a few days he wondered why the old man had given him no lessons, but continued to sit calmly under the tree while the young man made dinner and cleaned up after. At length the young man asked the master if the sword fighting lessons could start. Again the old many looked at him casually and asked him to say the words again. 'I would like to learn. I wish to be a great sword master and a skilled warrior'. Ah, replied the old man, if you are certain about this, then we will begin tomorrow.

But the next day continued like all the others, with one exception: while he was doing the cleaning the old man suddenly came up behind him from the bushes and hit him hard on the head with a pole. The young man grabbed his head in pain and watched the old master quickly scamper off into the bushes. He wondered if the old man had lost his mind, but as he had travelled so far and his desire was great, he simply returned to washing the dishes. At length this nightly head-bashing became like a ritual. For the first few weeks the young man simply endured the old master's eccentricity and carried on as before. But after a while, he became determined not to let the old man hit him. But he knew the old man was stealthy and clever and he would have to learn how to outwit him. Each night as he washed the dishes he learned to breathe very quietly. His ears became attuned to the slightest sound. He learned to wash the dishes without thinking and focused all his concentration on the sounds and the air of the night around him. He became capable of hearing the slightest crack of the tiniest twig. He was able to feel, just through the smallest change in the air around him, when the old man was getting near. He learned to judge, simply though the smell of the wooden pole, how close it was to him. And one night, miraculously, after many months of enduring the old man's behaviour, just as the pole was about to land on his head he shot his right arm up in a flash and caught the pole just a sliver of a second before the old man could strike him.

The old man released the wooden pole and came around to look at the young man. 'I see you are ready now', he said, and began to walk way into the night. 'But master!' cried the young man, 'what do you mean?' The old man turned around. 'You are ready to learn the art of the sword,' the old man replied. 'Up until this moment, you would have been so afraid of dying, you could never have been able to master the artistry of great swordsmanship'.[1]

The assessment

So what's it going to take?

Yes, that is the question. What will it take to get us to the point where we're not 'scared of dying' in the audition room? If we mean to take ourselves as seriously as dancers, musicians and athletes do, then we need to be honest with ourselves about what it's going to take. The point is to master what we do. As we've seen, the key to mastery is roughly ten years or 10,000 hours. If we analyse that, we might fairly conclude that we've done quite a lot of this work already. And of course, I'm not suggesting that we can't audition while we're working toward this mastery – in fact, auditioning itself is part of the plan. Most of my ex-students could safely say that they've put perhaps four to five years of work in. I'm suggesting that number, because most of them did a really intensive three-year programme, and in their lifetimes up until this point they've probably accumulated another one to two years. As we know, when we're not studying intensively, our experience tends to become sporadic: sometimes non-existent and sometimes intense if we're learning specific material for a specific audition or performance. But that isn't the way that most masterful musicians or athletes approach their study. They approach their training by having a set number of hours per day that they work at their art or their sport, and some identifiable targets or goals that they are aiming at in these sessions.

Let's take a musician for example. Standard advice is that practising more than four hours a day is actually detrimental. Of course, practising without thinking or without having a very clear and focused target in mind is a waste of time no matter how long you do it. Even dancers who aren't aiming for professional careers, but are focusing their studies on dance, spend between ten and sixteen hours in the studio per week. Again, it's important for dancers to be mindful of what they're doing as they practise so that they aren't simply going through the motions, or separating technique from imagination or a sense of artistry. Elite athletes train for six hours a day on average, but I think we can agree that this would be completely out of the question for singers or actors. The athlete's hours are this long because competing at an elite level requires that their training addresses muscles, skills and endurance in ways that acting or singing never would. However, even your average amateur runner, running for health or taking part in fun-runs, knows that it will take at least eight to twelve hours a week to keep themselves in shape.

So why is it that when I ask participants in the audition workshops I run how many hours they put in every day, the honest ones say that they don't think of performing in these terms? When they're rehearsing in a play they put in many hours every day, but when they aren't they don't put in *any* hours. They simply trust that the training they got at whatever drama school they went to is sufficient. They often have the feeling that if they're right for a part they'll get it and if they're not, they won't. In short, many tend to be fatalistic about the whole thing. However, others bring a bit of hubris to the process.

Earlier this year I was giving an audition workshop for some students at an FE College that prides itself on offering 'vocational' drama training to its students in a two-year programme. I was surprised to hear two of them describe themselves in an identical manner. 'I feel I have my craft in place,' they said. That struck me as a strange thing to hear from two young actors, neither of which could have been even twenty years old. I doubt if many mature actors could imagine describing themselves in this way. Part of the difficulty in imagining this would be to accept that when we're talking about performing we're talking about 'craft' as opposed to 'art'. Another difficulty might be in imagining that there are some kinds of testable indicators that allow us to make the judgement that we have 'our craft in place'. I can't imagine what those indicators would be, and I couldn't help but wonder how it was that the two actors had used that identical phrase. They were good examples of the kind of actor who feels that they are 'done', that they 'have their craft in place' and just need to get out and audition and take their chances. The more fatalistic actor often shares the feeling in these workshops that they will get the part if it's right for them. The overriding sentiment among these actors is an acceptance that the process is mysterious, out of their control, and that they can only do their best to present themselves as they are but always in the knowledge that they may not be what the panel is looking for. When I listen to these actors I sometimes think that I should start all audition workshops with the 'serenity prayer': 'Grant me the serenity to accept the things I cannot change, courage to change the things I can, and the wisdom to know the difference.'

We know that we can't change the curious and often idiosyncratic ways of the audition panel, but we can change what *we* do. Along with courage a practising performer needs passion and dedication in order to really change things, and so perhaps the 'serenity prayer' needs a small edit: 'Grant me the serenity to accept the things I cannot change, and the passion and dedication to change the things I can.' Without passion and dedication it's hard to imagine that any performer could get to the point where they aren't depending either on unwarranted confidence or some version of fatalism.

When the answer is 'I can't do anything' then we are in really big trouble. I suppose the one thing I think people need to realize is that we are in complete control of our lives. I can't ultimately control if they give me the part or not, but I can control everything about my performance, and I need to stay focused on what I can control. And generally in life if I do that I will end up having the success I am looking for. The first step is that people really do need stop thinking that they have no control over their lives, because frankly, it's just not true. It's only true if you believe it. There's a thing called expectancy theory: that which you focus on increases. So if I feel myself to be in a position where I don't have control, then I will absolutely have less control. But if I tell myself I can put my focus on controlling my performance, then I will actually have more control of my performance. You get more of what you focus on – whether that's negative or positive.

But the important thing to remember is that you have to have an achievement plan that matches your mental game. And everybody – whether they are performers or athletes – has absolute control over the work they put into achieving their goals.

Jason Selk

The important point to take away here is that a performer who has mastered their art might indeed have the power to change the mind of a casting panel – simply by making them see things differently. And they might be far better able to accept that there are things out of their control (like the whims of casting directors) if they know that they have controlled all that they can. I don't meet a lot of performers who feel this way, but then I rarely meet performers who can confidently say that they spend ten to twelve hours a week practising.

This is right at the heart of what this part of the book is about: if we want to have the kind of confidence that 'how-to-audition' books encourage us to display; if we want to feel like we are truly ready for anything that an audition panel can throw at us; and if we want to expect the world to take us seriously when we say that we intend to make a career of our performing, then we have to accept that without incredible luck (of the kind that very few people experience) our only chance of seriously attempting to make a living in this field is to *master it.*

What's going on here?

It's probably clear that most of us go into an audition room feeling like the young swordsman: so busy being 'scared of dying' that we can't focus on our art. The purpose in training to the point of mastery is to get beyond all that and find the artistry in what you do. We need to do what the young man in the story does: we need to get so alive and in tune technically with what we're doing that we can focus our attention on discovering the truly great part of our art. And that, of course, means that we have to develop a strategy for boosting our skill.

Before you can create a strategy for developing and improving your skills, you need to know where you are. You need to be able to figure out for yourself where you stand in relation to the demands of auditioning. The problem is that, as we've seen, we're not great at assessing ourselves – so where do we start?

I would suggest that we start by looking for patterns instead of at particular performances. The following exercises will enable you to identify patterns in your audition experience and help you get a grip on where you are. Once you have established what these patterns are you can try to determine if you want to change the pattern and what kind of changes you want to make. Before you start, read through these three interviews with actors who volunteered to go through this exercise for me:

Interview One

What's going on here?

Well, I keep going to auditions and getting down to the last few but never getting offered the job.

What does this make you?

It makes me the 'nearly' person. I nearly got big shows in the West End – I was down to the last two.

What might be the larger issue here?

Not sure – maybe I don't have that extra 'it' thing. I seem to create some kind of conflict in the minds of auditioning people. Often I get quite a few recalls and to me, that suggests that they can't make up their minds what to do with me.

What could that conflict be about?

I think I look a bit 'soft' in terms of how to cast me. I don't fit comfortably into the usual casting types. My playing range is probably 25–35, but I don't really look typical of my age. Somehow I think I look older.

Let's go back to the 'nearly' person. Are there other areas of your life where you feel like you're 'nearly' there?

Yes – I feel like I come close but somehow never really get on top of things. I nearly decide something but then don't follow through with it. I can be very indecisive.

So maybe 'nearly' is the pattern that we're seeing here. Can you think of things to do that might interrupt this pattern?

Well – to get something in the West End! But I guess you're talking about something I can do for myself. I guess I could stop beating myself up so much afterward. Every time I come close and then don't get it I put myself through a lot of hard criticism. I spend hours thinking how I didn't do this or that right; I just start focusing on all the things that could have made them go off me. That makes me slightly more desperate each time not to go through that beating myself up, so maybe I carry a little desperation into the room with me? Perhaps I can also just work at being more decisive generally about everything in my life!

If you were on the audition panel watching your last audition, what would your notes be?

- *Song not entirely secure (I was trying a new song – wasn't wholly confident)*

- *Look? Right age, but somehow looks a bit older?*
- *Friendly, confident*
- *Good cold reading*

So what do you want to change?

I want to make sure I'm not carrying any desperation into the room with me. I want to try and be more decisive about things and stop being afraid of making big decisions about what I want to do. And I want to be sure I don't do material that I secretly know isn't ready.

Interview Two

What's going on here?

My very last audition was for an advert campaign. I knew I wasn't right for the brief of 'preferably blonde and thin air hostess type'. I look Mediterranean and even having lost a lot of weight, I am curvy. I allowed myself to be defeatist before I entered the room, despite this casting agent having cast me in something the month before!

The couple of auditions before that were for two straight plays. I prepared well and felt strong. I got recalled for both. The directors, in both cases, seemed excited about me. I didn't get either job, and again, in both cases, I thought I could see the director's estimation of me deflate through the recall. Both recalls were workshops and were with other great actors. Later in the recall I allowed my admiration of these other actors to knock my confidence, even though I was called in numerous times to be seen with different groups.

What does that make you (if anything)?

I may be a person who psyches herself out? I find that the jobs I am not too fussed about getting, or am able to kid myself into thinking that I am not too fussed about getting, are the ones I get. With the ones that I really, really want, I allow myself to become doubtful of achieving that final yes! So perhaps I am 'the doubter' and in a recall the director sees that.

What might be the larger issue here (if any)?

I would rather have the control. Thinking that I've already failed before I'm told so by a casting agent or director, and attributing that to things like 'that person has more experience than me' or 'I am not the right shape' feels safer to me and puts me in control somehow. I guess fear of failure and, weirdly, fear of success may be the larger issues.

Are there other areas in your life that relate to your audition 'pattern'?

*I have battled with my weight for a very long time and often wonder if this is linked to the fear that I'll lose the weight but still not get the part. That would mean that the fault lies with my skills or talent and **not** an outside entity over which I have little control in the moment.*

Business ventures are really scary for me even though I know I have the skills to make these ventures work and I find the beginnings of them exciting. I recently received a decent grant toward one of my business ideas and am so much more anxious now as there are all these expectations that I must fulfil. I need to accept that failing is okay, and that I can only learn from it. One failure does not make up all of me. Just writing that was difficult!

If you were on the audition panel for your last audition, what would your notes be?

- *Worked well in a group, listened and took direction well*
- *Good comic timing and improv skills*
- *Lost confidence as the day went on; disappointing as we really liked her*
- *Didn't give me enough versatility*
- *Not quite as thin as we want for this part*

So what do you want to change?

I need to achieve stamina and a calm confidence in a long audition process. I want to recognise when I'm starting to doubt myself, to catch it early, and have practical things to do to help me find my focus again. Just telling myself "It's ok, you are just as good, you were recalled for a reason" is not enough.

I need to accept that although I have a fear of failure, I have had successes already. I need to stop feeling like I want to take control of the outcome of an audition before it's happened yet. But I think that I need to take control of my life right now. I need to stick with the decision to get fitter and to lose those final last pounds, because I am so close and starting to falter, and being the best that I can be is part of the job that I have chosen. All easier said than done.

I want to expand my horizons, and make work happen for myself so that when I go to my next audition, I will feel like a working actor and a creatively fulfilled individual. I think this will make me feel less intimidated by other actors waiting in the corridor that I respect and admire.

I want to be ready for any audition that crops up so that I am not rushed and feel as prepared as I can be.

Interview Three

What's going on here?

*I tend to sail through the initial rounds. I always begin the process feeling very confident and actually enjoy the mechanics of auditioning. More often than not I will make it to the final rounds then don't get the job for various reasons, including, too fat, thin, tall, not right for the mix. It always seems to be that I get the jobs that I really don't want. In the last year or two I have been lucky enough to be called in for some fantastic jobs – jobs that I **really** wanted. The pressure of this led to nerves so bad that my voice didn't hold up as it should have done. In the past, when younger I didn't have a problem with nerves at all – but as I've gotten older I've found that the nerves definitely creep in.*

My first agent out of drama school told me early on that I was 'niche' casting and would struggle for most of my young years to secure roles. I think that this has stuck in my subconscious and I tell myself that I won't get the job, no matter how far I get.

What does this make you?

Defeatist, bitter and ultimately lazy. Lately I probably haven't put in the work as far as preparation of material goes. I will question why I should bother spending my time and money on it when it will lead to nothing.

What might be the larger issue here?

I struggle with self-motivation and self-confidence. I am a major procrastinator. I am also a control freak and don't like feeling that something is out of my hands. I guess it can definitely be linked back to my teenage years. I have always struggled with my weight and had a very negative attitude toward my body. Pair that with the fact that I grew up in a small, northern and incredibly homophobic mining town. When I began to come to terms with my sexuality I was verbally bullied for a number of years about being gay and this led to me going from a very extrovert child to an acutely shy teenager.

Are there other areas in your life that relate to your audition 'pattern'?

My weight and relationship with food. Tried many times throughout my teens and twenties to lose weight and always after some initial success would fail. Would tell myself that my ideal body was unobtainable. Had an idea for a theatre company for many years and procrastinated for eight years due to fear of another failure.

So what changes could you make now that might break the pattern?

- *I need to learn to control my nerves and work at not letting it affect me physically (voice.)*
- *Catch myself in my 'shy' moments and not let them jeopardise the various opportunities that present themselves to me.*
- *See a psychiatrist! Deal with my issues with food and general confidence.*
- *Be more focused and work harder at getting things done – less procrastination.*
- *Meditate more – this has helped me through numerous difficult moments over the years*

I've included these interviews to give you an idea of how this exercise works and, hopefully, to help you in framing your own answers. This exercise helps a lot in trying to determine if there are any patterns in terms of your audition history, and what things you know you want to change.

EXERCISE ONE

Take some time with this and see if you can find any patterns to your audition experiences.

1. *Think back over your audition experiences – what's going on here?*

2. *What does that make you (if anything)?*
3. *What might be the larger issue here (if any)?*
4. *Are there other areas in your life that relate to your audition 'pattern'?*
5. *If you were on the audition panel for your last audition, what would your notes be?*
6. *So what changes could you make now that might break the pattern?*

EXERCISE TWO

At this point we also need to focus on how you feel about auditioning at the moment. Circle the three below that come closest to how you feel about auditioning right now:

Stuck	Confused	Capable
Challenged	Frightened	Excited
Powerless	Masterful	Confident
Excited	Overwhelmed	Prepared
	Anxious	

Your 'score':

If you have two negative and one positive: you're probably not enjoying the audition experience much and you might want to put some extra effort into the chapter on developing your mental game.

If you have two positive and one negative: you're probably in a fairly good place, but want to figure out how to get to a better score. You might be thinking that you want to improve the skills that you have and really master what you're doing. You will also want to really put some time into developing your mental game so that you can feel positive all the time about the experience.

If you have three positive feelings: you're probably wondering why you aren't cast more often and perhaps it's time to make sure that you've really developed your skills to the level that you need. You will probably want to focus much more on skill development, since you seem to have your mental attitude in the right place for auditioning.

If you have three negative feelings: then it's important for you to recognise how crucial it is for you to work on your mental game, as this may affect your audition experience no matter how strong your actual abilities may be.

How good am I?

Hopefully you've identified a pattern in your audition experience and also pinpointed what your feelings are about auditions in a very general way (yes, I know, that would make a good book on its own). But how can you assess where you are in terms of skill level? As we've seen, we're not the best judge of ourselves. Some of you may be in training, or have just been in training, so you probably have a very good idea of what your strengths are and what you still need to develop. But how about those of us who are just adrift out here on our own? How do we figure out where we are in terms of where we want to be? I would suggest that this is the point at which you want to find a 'critical friend'. That phrase is an interesting one: some of us already have a lot of critical friends and might not feel that we need to look for any more! But the critical friend is important – you need someone who cares about you but is also willing to be honest. Ideal people would be ex-tutors, people that you know in the business whose judgement you trust, or friends who take this business seriously.

EXERCISE THREE

One way to get some sense of how we see ourselves is through a simple comparison. This exercise is purely subjective and is designed to see how you think you sit alongside your ideal performer. For this exercise, think about performers whose work you know and admire. There may be a lot of different kinds of performers that come to mind, but just allow yourself to think of those whose work, for one reason or another, you really like.

Now try to sift through all of those possibilities and choose one that you most admire and whose work you would most like to emulate in your own. Once you have that person in mind, score them from 1–10 in each area: the first five are important, but only fill in the ones that matter to you out of the second five. Here is a sample of this, filled in by a volunteer:

My ideal performer:

1. *Voice/vocal skill*	7
2. *Physical skill*	7
3. *Creativity/risk factor*	10
4. *Charisma/confidence*	10
5. *Conviction/believability*	10
6. *Warmth/engaging quality*	10
7. *Eccentricity/uniqueness*	7
8. *Transformational ability*	9
9. *Intelligence/knowledge*	8
10. *Look (of whatever kind)*	8

Me:

1. *Voice/vocal skill*	8
2. *Physical skill*	6
3. *Creativity/risk factor*	8
4. *Charisma/confidence*	9
5. *Conviction/believability*	7
6. *Warmth/engaging quality*	10
7. *Eccentricity/uniqueness*	7
8. *Transformational ability*	6
9. *Intelligence/knowledge*	8
10. *Look (of whatever kind)*	8

I know the actor who filled this in and, as 'her critical friend' reading over the list, I would say that there are some scores that seem right and some that could use a little more consideration. This actor has a tremendous singing voice, so I can see why the score of 8 is here for her voice/vocal skill. But I would suggest that her speaking voice could still use a lot of work, particularly in feeling comfortable losing her regional accent and in getting a more centred, rich and resonant sound. I would have scored at a 5/6 for voice/vocal skill. Charisma seems right at 9 but confidence does not – I would have said 5. But apart from that I think the scoring is about right here.

Now it's your turn. Once you've gone through the exercise and scored your 'ideal' performer, go through the list again and score yourself against the first five and against the ones that matter to you out of the second five:

Ideal performer:

1. *Voice/vocal skill*
2. *Physical skill*
3. *Creativity/risk factor*
4. *Charisma/confidence*
5. *Conviction/believability*
6. *Warmth/engaging quality*
7. *Eccentricity/uniqueness*
8. *Transformational ability*
9. *Intelligence/knowledge*
10. *Look (of whatever kind)*

Me:

1. *Voice/vocal skill*
2. *Physical skill*
3. *Creativity/risk factor*
4. *Charisma/confidence*
5. *Conviction/believability*
6. *Warmth/engaging quality*
7. *Eccentricity/uniqueness*
8. *Transformational ability*
9. *Intelligence/knowledge*
10. *Look (of whatever kind)*

Of course, this is a very 'unscientific' exercise, but that doesn't really matter. However subjective, these views will be informing how you feel about yourself and that in turn will affect your progress. Now, *run this assessment past your critical friend.* In fact, if you can, run it by a few critical friends, and find out if they agree or disagree with your assessment.

Once you have a score level in all areas, you should have an idea of how you think you compare to your sort of 'ideal'. The advantage of this exercise is that even though it is very much about your own aesthetic judgement in terms of performing, it gives you a lot to think about in terms of how you view both your sense of the 'ideal' performer and your sense of what your own strengths and weaknesses are. From this fairly simple start, you can begin to make a blueprint for your skills development plan.

Approaching the work

When we're talking about putting in ten to twelve hours a week, we know that we've got to keep things challenging and interesting. There's no other way to approach this without almost guaranteeing our own failure. Of course, you are in control here, but I would think that in an ideal world, training time would be split between technical things: voice, movement, fitness, cold reading, interview technique and broader, less tangible areas like play, creativity, imagination, expressivity and analysis.

Because it's generally easier to set goals for work in technical areas, I would suggest starting there. There are many books available that have already done the hard work for you (they present tried and tested exercises) and can help you plan this part of your work effectively and relatively easily. The resources section at the back of this book will help you find some great exercises and training plans that have been designed by some of the very best minds in the business.

To get a sense of how this might work with the sample Exercise Three above, let's go back and look at what the subject's high and low technical scores were against her ideal. Clearly, she thinks she needs more work in the areas of physical skill (and knowing her, I would say she includes fitness in this). She also needs – according to me, her 'critical friend' – speech and text work. These first two areas are clearly technical: voice and movement/fitness. In creating her work plan, she can start by going through the resources section in the back of this book and deciding where she wants to start in terms of books/exercises for voice and movement, and of course, any time spent in the gym or working out at home will be part of her ten to twelve hours a week.

The next two areas – transformational ability and conviction/ believability – are less purely technical and more related to imagination and creativity. These areas are also well-covered in a number of very helpful books, and the first stop in making a working plan would be to check out those parts of the resources section at the back of the book that address imagination and transformation. However, I would suggest that you should also be pursuing creativity in a unique and self-designed way.

New ways to work, play and create

When we're looking at the 'intangibles' like charisma, creativity, risk, uniqueness, transformational ability, etc., we have to find things for ourselves that encourage our sense of play. You can't always find this in a book. Playing is much more important and much more significant in terms of learning than it sounds. If we aren't careful we might be in danger of turning our ten to twelve hours' weekly practice time into *work*, and I think this is especially true if we take everything out of a book.

Much of our motivation to do anything comes from the amount of pleasure that we calculate we might derive from it. There's no point even thinking about doing ten or twelve hours of practice/rehearsal/ training per week if we don't think that it will be pleasurable. This means that, from the very start, it's important to think in terms of how we can use our dedicated practice time to get down to the serious business of *play*.

Start a revolution

We know that there's a whopping great part of your brain that works away unconsciously. This part of the brain has been called the 'cognitive unconscious'. The cognitive unconscious is a lot more tyrannical than you might think. It is, in fact, a bit of a bully and a self-appointed autocrat. It grabs for itself the lion's share of decision-making. This isn't down to arrogance or aspiration, but simple efficiency. We can't actually attend to every little detail of being alive. We would go mad if we had to consciously attend to every decision from breathing, blinking and adjusting the dilation of our pupils to varying light intensities, to distinguishing a cereal box by colour/shape/size and then estimating the distance of our hand to the spoon, then from spoon to mouth, etc. This is only a tiny fraction of what our cognitive unconscious is busy doing for us at breakfast. It is so smoothly efficient at these tasks that it leaves us free to read and start an argument over a *Sunday Times* editorial. So far so good. But we pay a very heavy price for that efficiency when it comes to creative decisions, as Gregory Berns points out:

> The evolutionary theory of perception, coupled with the efficiency of the brain, means that perception is a statistical process. For any given [stimuli] the brain must choose one of several possible interpretations. Efficiency dictates that *the brain will pick the most likely interpretation* ... The interpretation may be guided by past experience and how the individual categorizes people and objects.[2]

Categorisation is, in itself, one of the great enemies of creativity and also serves to inhibit risk. The presentation of 'the most likely interpretation' is what makes so much acting so dull. In order to add a level of risk into our work we need to fight our natural inclination to categorise, and find some definite strategies that will inspire us to play, innovate and create. We need to consciously develop the ability to suspend judgement, and to consider without categorising. Learning to absorb information without interpreting is critical to creativity and requires concentrated focus. The danger, of course, is that once focused we tend to draw on our logical faculties. At that point we tend to do consciously what our cognitive unconscious does so well: we will choose the most likely interpretation. The only way to fight back is to create a little revolution and topple the regime of conscious or unconscious categorisation, and all logical, likely interpretations.

When we're working, learning and rehearsing to master our art, we need to acknowledge the serious limitation of approaching it all with the usual trappings of logic and the desire to be right. The problem is that the older we get, the harder we have to work to fight our own brain's efficiency, and the more we tend to rely on likely interpretations. This is why adults generally only use chairs to sit in, while children use them to build forts or make tunnels. In fact, because children don't have the weight of experience to guide interpretation they are much freer from the burdens of categorisation. In general, as the years go by, we start to believe that learning should be methodical, serious and logical:

> As we grow older, we are taught that learning should be serious, that subjects are complicated. These serious subjects take serious study we are told, and play only trivializes them. And yet learning all the complications of a subject first can be confusing and dispiriting ... Sometimes the best way to get the feel of a complicated subject is to just play with it. That's why kids often learn computer systems faster than adults – they aren't afraid to just try stuff out and see what works, whereas adults worry that they will do something wrong. Kids don't fear doing something wrong. If they do, they learn from it and do it differently next time. Learning and memory also seem to be fixed more strongly and last longer when learned in play.[3]

There's a lot for us to think about in here – not least how we can sometimes let audition fears convince us that there is a right or wrong in the world of artistic expression. But the research into the ways in which play can boost memory is also important for us.

Why play is critical

Stuart Brown, a psychiatrist and clinical researcher who has made a lifetime study of play, concludes that 'the genius of play is that, in playing, we create imaginative new cognitive combinations. And in creating those novel combinations, we find what works'.[4] In a sense it may seem a strange thing to have to consider the idea of 'play' when we're talking about acting. Surely the whole essence of performing *is* play. Actors are called 'players' and they 'play' roles; singers 'play' roles when they sing – so why should we even need to consider the importance of play when we're thinking about how to increase our time spent in disciplined and focused rehearsal? One answer is simple enough, and emerges from Brown's statement above: being playful is about creating imaginative new thought-combinations. Another is that during the hard work of performing (and between text-analysis and memorisation, physical and vocal exercise and conditioning there is much of it), we need to remember that when it comes to creating inspired, beautiful, risky and engaging performing we can't rely on logic alone. Of course, when we talk about putting in a lot of hours, we are likely to be more inspired if we describe those hours as being dedicated to play than if we describe them to being dedicated to work. As such, on the level of motivation alone it's important that we (at least partly) think of the time we put into developing our performance skills as focused and dedicated *playing* time.

But what is play? And why should it have to be explained to a performer? The first question isn't as easy to answer as it looks. Play – rather like imagination, to which it is closely linked – is easier to do than to explain. This is apparent from the reluctance with which Stuart Brown undertakes the task of defining play (he is reluctant because, rather like a good joke, 'analysing it takes the joy out of it'), and this reluctance comes from a man whose life work has been to study it. In the end, he doesn't really define play, but settles for outlining the 'properties of play':

> Apparently purposeless (done for its own sake)
> Voluntary
> Inherent attraction

Freedom from time
Diminished consciousness of self
Improvisational potential
Continuation of desire[5]

I am talking here of play with a purpose, so the very first property of play as he describes it is perhaps compromised by the idea of play as serving a purpose (unless we remember that not all of the play we will do in rehearsal *has* to serve a purpose). I would suggest that one could spend many hours playing *as* Hamlet in a variety of situations – on the tube, in Tesco, at a restaurant – and while none of these play scenarios has to be without purpose it may well be that, in the end, specific play scenarios were not in themselves purposeful. However, the fact that play is voluntary, attractive, free, unself-conscious, improvisational and a continuation of desire is *exactly* what makes it valuable to performers.

Importantly, play is both something we're hardwired to do, and something that we don't have to *force* ourselves to do: we generally love to play when given the opportunity. Play inspires us, recreates us and gives us pleasure. For these reasons, seeing our dedicated rehearsal time as a time of true and dedicated play is a great way to keep ourselves motivated.

Because we so often start our rehearsals with a logical premise, learning to play sometimes means trying to defy that logic. Overall, what we really need to do through play is find ways to avoid the 'likely interpretation'. The likely interpretation comes from categorising which, as Gregory Berns points out, is 'death to imagination'.[6] While we're in our usual environment we grow used to categorising things. This is why, when we travel, we often have heightened emotional and imaginative responses to what we experience. Time seems different, things suddenly spark memories or ideas, and we tend to be much more open to rethinking and reinterpreting the world around us.

As performers, we need to make sure that we have these kinds of opportunities as often as possible. Some of the simplest ways to do this is to make sure that you're switching up your environment as often as you can. This doesn't require travel to exotic locations (although that would be nice too), but could be something as simple as changing your daily travel route, or consciously switching the order of your usual morning routine. Anything that moves you away from your habitual actions can be a positive step. Take time on your weekends to do things you've never done, and when you do, make sure you're really exploiting the change by paying attention to the newness and what it might inspire in your imagination.

> What is risk? Is that having faith in your own ideals? There is a faith in your own talents; there is a faith that you have to perform. I love a risky audition. I love the person who has their own ideas. I like people who have their own ideas about who the character is or what the character does. Sometimes it's interesting to see people who think they're right for a part when we don't. I get agents calling and saying so-and-so wants to be seen for this part, and I say I don't think they're right – do you think they're right? Actors will always think that they're right for things that they're not. It's very rare that an actor knows where they sit in our world. But sometimes, when an actor feels sure and has a certain energy; they walk into a room, they're alive, they're kicking and I can only describe them as quite chipper. They have a kind of courage that maybe comes from thinking they're right for this, and if they can be clear about what they're doing, then that risk; that 'chipper energy' can pay off. And I think 'maybe they are right'. When they do their audition there's a twinkle in their eye, there's a joy in doing it that makes it all work.
>
> David Grindrod

Surely play has got to be the thing that brings joy into our work, and the more we can do it, the better the chance that we can bring some of that joy into even the scariest audition room. Here are some simple suggestions that will help you to combine experimenting with new places/routines and imaginative play when you begin to make a plan for your work:

Visual starting points:
- Visit a gallery you've never been to. Choose a portrait of any kind and write/improvise a short monologue or song based on

it. Always work from a point of view that is the opposite of your first impression. (If the portrait looks like a wealthy woman, perhaps you will imagine that she is cleaning lady who has stolen the clothes?)

- Chose a piece of abstract art and find or write a short monologue or song based on it. Perhaps the wilder the art, the more conservative the monologue/song?

Observational starting points:

- Spend an afternoon at a train station or airport and take notes on what you see that sparks your imagination. Write/improvise short monologues, scenes or songs based on things you observed that really intrigued you. Write against your first impressions – if you think you're seeing an accountant, imagine you're seeing a hustler.
- Choose a place of natural beauty that you've never visited and work on any of your portfolio pieces there. Let the environment really affect meaning, sound and feel. Don't let logic get in the way of this.

Musical starting points:

- Take a piece of music you've never heard before (instrumental is easiest) and work a piece of text against it. This could be a cold reading, lyrics or a monologue you know. Be moved by the music only.
- Find a new piece of music that influences how you walk, sit or move and imagine basing a character on the music. Keep logic out of this exercise.

Working against type:

- Find a role that, in your opinion, would be the least logical casting for you and begin serious work on it in a playful way. Starting purely in your own imagination or from any of the above points take on something you think is *completely* wrong for you. Once you've found this cast-against-type role, think of a place that they might go to and visit. Start your work on the role in this new place (perhaps a bank lobby or small café). Don't worry about text at this point, but simply try to recreate their body in this new, unfamiliar place. Really play with and exaggerate the kind of transformational choices you have to make: the exercise will make you think not only of the way in which you type-cast yourself, but might also make you rethink what you want to do, or can do, about that.

- Take some of the things you put into your illogical casting exercise and apply them to a piece of material that you're already working on that you think *is* the right casting for you. No matter how illogical, just apply anyway and see what you learn.

Never waste a journey:

- Whenever you're travelling, keep notes. Watch, observe and imagine being the people you see that are the most intriguing to you. Record your 'likely categorisation' of the person and then imagine that they are completely different from that. Work out their rough life story while you're travelling and then work out details when you have practice time. Start first by trying to really imitate their movement, gesture and expression. Try writing a brief biography or song about the person exactly as you think they are.
- Write a short monologue or song for them and make it ridiculously melodramatic. Imagine where they're going, where they've been, what's about to happen to them, etc. Imagine why they don't look like a typical example of whatever it is you've decided they are.

I had an actor who came in one day and he told me he was taking an intensive summer class at one of the most respected conservatoires in New York. But he really wasn't finding it helpful. What he did find helpful was riding the subways.

Ellen Lewis

- Do a 'Sherlock': starting from their shoes, move upwards and gather as many clues as you can. Focus on the really contradictory ones (expensive shoes/cheap bag; young person/'old' style, clean hands/filthy clothes, etc.) and construct a narrative around the contradiction.

Here are some things you can do while staying in familiar environments:

Choreograph a monologue or song:

- Don't do this in a demonstrative way and don't use gestures. Don't even use text or lyrics: just find some music that has a resonance of some kind with a monologue or lyric you love, and choreograph whatever movements seem to connect to both your heart and your monologue or song (don't use the actual song music: find something else). Don't rush this – really play with it.
- Go back to the text after playing with movement for a couple of hours and see if you can find something new in it. Try to let your body, and not your head, find the new things.

Cold read strange things:

- Take newspaper editorials, instruction manuals, or advert copy and cold read as a character of some sort. This could be a character you've played in the past, or you could start from any of the ideas above. You could read as someone you've observed, as a portrait you liked or as the character you would never be cast as. Even though it's likely to sound absurd (especially in the case of instruction manuals), just enjoy giving life and character to the text.
- Cold read published diaries. This is most effective if you can find some pictures of someone who is *nothing like* the writer. Enjoy feeling as if you're really getting into the world of both text and picture (which might be greatly at odds). Try to bring them together in your reading.

Work against your likely interpretations of characters:
- Use the following list: a teapot, a brick, a dried flower, a morning paper, an oak tree, a favourite chair, a well-worn pathway, a missing glove, an overfull bag, a flimsy fence, an open door, a flickering candle, a half-read book, an abstract painting. Choose two that interest you and write two paragraphs on any chosen character, each beginning with: 'Othello (or whatever you've chosen) is like an overfull bag . . .'
- Write a brief paper describing either your own character or your character's 'character' from the point of view of one person who loves you deeply and one person who hates you absolutely.

Always be writing something:
- Use any of these ideas listed and make sure that you're always thinking about writing something. Not only does it give you something to talk about in interviews, it could lead to other possibilities. It will stretch your imagination, keep you thinking about dramatic structure and extend your story-telling abilities.

Exploring the 'unlikely'

People who write about processes for increasing creativity tend to centre on the importance of clearly defining your problem. For example, actors usually do this in a methodical way. We generally begin by asking questions such as: Who is Ophelia? What does she want? What do other people say about her? What are her obstacles? What are her relationships? And so on. In other words, our creative problem tends to be two-fold. The first is to investigate a text fully in order to understand what is there, and also to explore and be creative about what is *not* there. Once we think we've done enough initial exploration, we're ready to move on to the second element and explore the creative problem in a practical way by bringing things to life in rehearsal and performance.

In these early stages of exploring possible risky performance decisions we have to be sure we've given ourselves enough time to explore the margins. Sometimes it helps to think in terms of simple opposites. Sometimes it helps to think of the *worst* possible idea and play with it. Remember that you're trying to experiment with whatever will lead you away from the 'likely interpretation'.

Let's take look at Ophelia as a case study of playing with simple opposites. Before we can do this, we have to spend time reading the play and analysing Ophelia's character and actions, and then make a list of things that describe her. For example, at various points in the play one could reasonably describe Ophelia as:

> Young
> Frightened
> Confused
> Sheltered
> In love
> Mentally fragile
> Religious
> Obedient
> A virgin

But what happens when you swap one thing on the list for its opposite? Well, young is hard to swap for old, but the rest could give you some risky and more interesting starting points:

- *Frightened* could be swapped for *bold*: she is bold enough to return her brother's advice and bold enough to return Hamlet's gifts.
- *Confused* for *certain*: she knows how badly Hamlet has behaved toward her and feels certain that she knows how court politics work.
- *Sheltered* for *worldly*: she clearly knows what kind of mischief Laertes might get into as he departs and she also seems to know some bits of surprisingly bawdy song when she comes back in her 'mad' appearance.
- *In love* for *not in love*: she certainly gives Hamlet up easily enough at her father's suggestion.

- *Mentally fragile* for *very sharp*: is she really mad? The question is usually applied to Hamlet but Ophelia has good reason to come in and 'haunt' Gertrude with feigned madness: after all, Gertrude witnessed her son killing her father. Ophelia's 'mad' speech has references to an old dead man and flowers that speak of memory: is this madness a subtle and safe way of letting Gertrude know that she is wise to what happened?
- *Religious* for *atheist*: in her grief at her father's death she never really mentions anything that might suggest religious devotion.
- *Obedient* for *disobedient*: see below.
- *A virgin* for *experienced*: there is good reason to read the inclusion of her song about the man who would not marry the woman who slept with him in the 'mad' scene as her explanation of why Hamlet rejected her.

Of course, it isn't that these things will never have been considered by others, it is simply that the first list forms part of what I would consider (after many years of watching Ophelia's speeches in audition) to be part of 'the likely interpretation'. My point is that the 'opposites' exercise leads us into much more interesting territory for exploration. This exercise gives us a lot to play with in terms of who Ophelia is or might be. But what about what Ophelia wants? Most performances of Ophelia I've ever seen seem to suggest that she wants to marry Hamlet and please her father and her brother. But again, before you start your practical work, you could very profitably begin by asking whether those things are true.

Stay open to the process

Whenever you're exploring new and risky things, you need to allow yourself to explore everything – even the absurd – and to suspend judgement for as long as you can. Try not to censor or block ideas as they come up, and make sure you're patient with your exploration. Remember that your goal is to try and work against what comes quickly, which means acknowledging that what you're after is what comes slowly. Of course, working with illogical or unexpected ideas won't solve all of the problems that a text might set you, so what you're really after here is finding out how to incorporate some of your explorations of the margins into your more logically deduced work. As actors, most of us know the feeling of trying something new and knowing that it simply feels right or wrong. Often we rely on this instinct to help us make choices about what we do. While that instinct can be important, it can also be the product of habit. Make sure that before you come to any quick decisions you've given yourself adequate time to explore even the most unlikely ideas. The kind of risks that pay off come from real and sustained exploration, coupled with great skill in expression. The whole process ultimately requires the kind of mastery that will give us confidence and strengthen our nerve when we're thinking about going out on a limb.

Of course, the exercises described above are not the usual 'practise my monologue/song' exercises, because they are specifically *not* about *direct* practice but about stretching imagination and creativity. Only choose things that really speak to your playful side: only you can know what sparks your imagination, so consider this basic list as just an example of the things that you could be exploring in your ten to twelve hours a week. The most important things to get out of these exercises are an awareness of how quickly you categorise something and then the experience of playing with all the exotic, unusual and opposite possibilities you can find – no matter how illogical.

Think differently about what constitutes practice

I've been suggesting this all along, but you need to learn to think differently about what makes up your practice time before you can start planning it. This is where acting differs mightily from activities such as ballet, violin lessons or 100-metre hurdles. Much of our work is spent on tangible outcomes such as learning, researching, rehearsing text, acquiring new skills and enhancing our physical abilities, but for the creative, interpretive artist more is needed. Enhancing your knowledge of history, art, literature, music, psychology, philosophy, classical mythology – the list goes on! – is part of what makes up your creative arsenal and is massively influential in the choices you make as a performer. To paraphrase a fairly well-known quotation: 'What do they know of performing, who only performing know?' Nothing will fuel your motivation more than a curiosity about nearly everything. And the moment you can truly recognise what tireless curiosity can do for your preparation is probably the moment when all this practice begins to feel incredibly exciting. It means that while you're thinking about formulating a structured plan for your work you need to be thinking in broad terms about how you collect, use and synthesise knowledge for your own greater good.

This is where allowing yourself to follow your curiosity is important, although this is difficult to legislate and plan for (and even more difficult for someone else to plan for you). Instead, you need to remain open to how one exploration leads to another, always linking that exploration to specific goals. In a terrific book called *The Secrets of a Buccaneer-Scholar* James Bach outlines some useful questions for when you're in the exploration part of your work:

> As I live and learn, I stumble into some idea or technique that may help me solve an authentic problem. Learning about that idea leads me to more ideas as I ask myself questions:
>
> * What are examples of this idea?
> * How might this idea help me?
> * Are there other ideas like this one?
> * Where do I go to study this idea in detail?
> * How can I [put this idea into] practice right now?[7]
>
> And:
>
> * Anything I learn is a gateway to everything else I will ever know.[8]

So, with these things in mind I can't help but urge you to be creative about how you go about all of this. If you get it right, it won't feel quite the same as a rigid four-hours-a-day violin practice, nor will it be like sweating it out in a gym four to five hours a day. In a sense, it will be about searching. It will be about endless curiosity. It will be about creatively synthesising knowledge, asking absurd questions and then spending some time trying to figure out if there might be an answer.

Ways to combine work and social life

Start a support network/group

This is the most powerful thing you can do to keep yourself on track. It will give you a place to cultivate critical friends that you respect, support each other's work and try out new material. If you can set up a support group and commit to regular meetings (once a month? perhaps twice in the first couple of months?), you'll find out what members of Weight Watchers and Alcoholics Anonymous have known for years: that working with a group strengthens your commitment, gives you a positive sounding board and a place to share experiences, and helps to keep you going when you hit tough moments. Most performers have a lot of other friends who are performers and a lot of them have free time as they work in flexible jobs to support their audition opportunities. Getting together with others will help you stick to your plans and inspire your colleagues to stick to theirs as well.

This is also invaluable in terms of feedback. As you work, you need feedback to help you gauge your progress. Getting feedback from just one person that you trust is helpful, but getting feedback from more than one person (as long as you trust them) is even better. Your group can also help you in practising under pressure: just having to perform in front of an audience, however informal, is a pressure and the more often you can work under pressure the better you'll handle it when it matters.

See more theatre/arts

Once a week see a performance. Go with friends if you can, and have a long discussion about what you saw afterwards. If you live in or near a big city this is often possible to do relatively cheaply. Find drama-school productions or get preview tickets. If live theatre isn't available or isn't a financial option, go and see a good film. Concentrate on one actor and write out a review afterward: what you loved, what worked, what surprised you, how you might have interpreted the role differently, etc.

See an exhibition

Go with friends to see an exhibition in a museum or gallery and discuss what you thought of it afterwards. Alternatively, go on your own and use the experience to approach the creative exercises listed earlier in this chapter.

Go to a concert

It is especially beneficial to attend concerts that feature the kinds of music that you never listen to. While there, think your way through some text that you're working on, or concentrate on a particular character you're working on. Don't bring your logical mind into this: let the music do all the 'thinking' for you.

Other things to do

Think long term and take on a big project

I once decided in grad school that I was tired of everyone knowing Shakespeare's work extensively when I didn't, so I spent a year reading the plays and then watching BBC videos of them (these were available in my university library). I didn't manage to read and see a play every week – sometimes I only read the play and watched the video the following week. I seem to recall that it took me most of the year to get through all of the plays, but the confidence it gave me in knowing the repertoire was priceless.

You could make a similar decision, or go for other writers that you really want to tackle. You could also take on a bigger project like really mastering one physical technique. You could decide to devote a year to taking Tai Chi classes, which are great for strength, stillness and concentration. Or you could just decide to spend a year reading as much Greek drama and any accompanying mythology as possible. Not only would it give you a great classical grounding, but you would suddenly feel more confident about all those classical allusions in plays and paintings.

Go to a lot of auditions

Take on as much as you can. Practising your pre-, auditioning and post-auditioning routine is all part of the work and the more you can do the better you'll get. Don't audition for things you wouldn't take – you'll only get a reputation for being a frivolous auditionee – but don't be shy about attending things you haven't done before, like open calls.

Give up 'perfectionism'

Whenever I meet someone who tells me they're a perfectionist I know that what they're really telling me is they're afraid. If you endlessly chase after something that really doesn't exist, then you are in fact running away from the fear of failing or the fear of being criticised for failing. Fear drives us into some strange places. It can make us decide that when we perform there are endless problems in our performance. It can make us focus constantly on what is *wrong* with us, it can keep our concentration on problems instead of solutions, and it can keep us in a permanent state of dissatisfaction with ourselves.

But it does have some 'up' sides. It allows us to stop negative criticism, because we get our 'pre-emptive strike' in first. In other words, there's no point in telling me that I wasn't very good because I'm already preoccupied with beating myself up. It can also mean that you are forever *right* when you decide that you're just not achieving perfection in that Juliet monologue. It also allows us to focus rather selfishly on ourselves all the time: we can't be worried about anyone or anything else because we're so busy worrying about ourselves. As you can see, the 'up' sides aren't terrific. So give it up. Work with joy instead. Work with the expectation of getting better and of continually learning from things no matter whether you're learning from the things that go well or learning from the things that go wrong.

Work endlessly on your portfolio

I can tell you from experience how disheartening (and how alarmingly common) it is to watch someone walk in with a huge portfolio of material and then go through it as if they're looking for something they want to do. Surely you should want to do *everything* in your portfolio? I've also watched many people who make what I call the 'fake offer'. In other words, someone asks 'What would you like to do today?' and they answer 'Well, I've got A or B'. As soon as someone says 'Great, let's hear B', I watch their faces fall as they say something along the lines of 'Well, A is really better for me'. Surely you should only offer what makes you sound great? Yes, yes, I know, I'm verging on the 'bleeding obvious' territory here, but because we're about to think up some practice plans I have to say it: *your portfolio is critical.*

It is more important than you think and it will take longer to compile than you might guess. Once you have it, you can never work on it too much. You need to keep it fresh, and you need to make sure that every piece is ready to do.

For me people fall into two groups. There are people who walk in and audition brilliantly. They're well prepared and they do a craftsmanlike audition. And then there are people who when they walk in I know what they're going to sing. When you've been doing this as long I have you just recognize them and you know that they're going to do the same material they always have. They don't adapt. They do that terrible thing where they walk in and say 'oh, I know it isn't exactly appropriate but I thought this song would be a good choice for this show', and I think 'no you didn't, you've brought this song because this is the song you've been doing for 20 years', you know? They've been doing this song for the whole of their career and they're going to cling to it like it's their lucky mascot and they'll be doing the song until the day they die. I always say you need an absolute minimum of 6 songs in different styles to get through in auditions – an absolute minimum of 6! – and if you don't loathe every single one of them, they're not ready. Your audition songs should absolutely drive you crazy because you've worked and worked and worked them. I love people who have a go at doing something new because they've found something that is particularly appropriate for the show I'm casting – but it isn't wise. Because it won't be sung into the voice; you're unlikely to have the measure of it – I just think I like to see people that I know have been constantly working at that portfolio of work. It always takes so much more work than people think.

Trevor Jackson

New ways to learn

Part of your plan will no doubt be to increase your repertoire of material. This alone can take substantial amounts of time out of your ten to twelve hours per week: especially if all the exercises and reading you've done so far have inspired you to completely refresh and rethink some of your material. Because we're looking at audition, it is worth thinking carefully about how you set about learning material in terms of using it in this specific context. Auditions are a completely unnatural situation: it's very hard to connect to an audition monologue in the same way as you might connect to a part with which you've had a full rehearsal period and performance run. While it's important that we think very hard about the kind of ways in which we approach learning *all* material, it's particularly important to think about how we learn *audition* material because we will be performing it in the highest pressure situation there is.

All of which means that how we learn and remember audition material in the first place is of critical importance. Let's take a moment to think about the pressure our brains are under when we're in an audition situation. If we begin to worry at all (and no matter how good our mental preparation is, there can be any number of unexpected things that can take up brain space through worrying), we use up part of what Sian Beilock has called 'cognitive horsepower'. This is her term for the working memory that helps you keep in mind all the information you need to negotiate an activity, while also serving as the 'command centre' of thought. As she points out:

> When pressure-filled situations create an inner monologue of worries in your head that taps verbal brain power, performing activities that also rely heavily on these same verbal resources is more difficult. Doing two things at once that rely on similar brain regions is generally harder than doing two things that call on separate pools of brain power.[9]

By way of demonstration she looks at how something as simple as switching a maths problem from this format:

$$32 - 17 =$$

to this format:

$$\begin{array}{r} 32 \\ -\underline{17} \end{array}$$

changes the part of the brain we use to solve it. In the first, horizontal, problem we tend to work on it as if we were reading a line of text, left to right, using our 'verbal' brain. In the second, vertical problem, we tend to use the spatial part of our brain for solving the problem.[10]

This has inspired me to think hard about how we might rethink some of our learning processes and about how we retrieve text under pressure. Auditions require that we retrieve text that we've learned using our 'verbal' brain centre. But if we're worried, or even if we're thinking strong positive thoughts in an audition room, this worried/positive thinking is bound to be competing with the cognitive horsepower that we need for text retrieval – and this, of course, is a recipe for choking under pressure. Beilock recommends 'cognitive outsourcing' to avoid overtaxing the verbal part of your brain. She writes about this specifically in terms of mathematical problems, but it occurs to me that performers have a similar 'overtaxing' problem with text retrieval.

While working recently on a television show called *Popstar to Operastar*, we were faced with long lines of text in a foreign language that had to be learnt at speed. I decided that this was the perfect opportunity to test the idea of learning through the visual/spatial area of the brain and not the verbal area and, interestingly enough, the visual/spatial exercise made an incredible difference to the ability to recall word-order. The interesting thing is that the parts of text that I remembered in the usual ways fled from my memory quickly (only a few weeks out from the final show) but the text that I 'drew' remains very vivid in my memory.

We were working on the *Anvil Chorus* and the first few lines go very quickly:

Vedi le fosche notturne spoglie de' cieli sveste l'immensa volta
Sembra una vedova che alfin si toglie i bruni panni ond'era
   involta

My first step was to write this out in a way that made sense to me phonetically:

Vaydee le fosskay noturnay spolye de chaylee svesta limmensa
   volta
Sembruna vaydova keyallfin see tolye ee brunee panee ondaira
   involta

I then drew separate pictures that came to represent the sounds of each line (things like fossils with keys, knots turning, spools, vests, lightning bolts, etc.). It took a bit of time, but once I had it I stopped looking at the typed-out text as I rehearsed and simply went through the pictures with the music. As I had to teach the piece to all of the popstars, as well as to the chorus, I felt that I had to know it very well myself and didn't want to be referring to the text or the music as I taught. The fact is that I don't read music well, so when I have to teach people who do read well (as our show chorus did) I become very nervous indeed. Consequently, this test of my 'visual recall' system was made under high-pressure circumstances.

The more ways you learn something, the more likely you will be able to retrieve it when you need to (like when you are auditioning). The idea is that every new way you learn something (or even in every new place you learn something) you add cues to what you learn (we call them retrieval cues) that can be used to help remember the information on audition day. For instance, let's say you have to memorize lines for an audition. If you only learn these lines by repeating them aloud and only practice them in your bedroom, when you get to the audition you will likely have more trouble recalling the lines than if you practice the lines in your bedroom, at a cafe, in the park and by not only repeating them, but by moving to them, singing, visualizing etc. This is because everywhere you practice (and every way you practice) you likely link some new thing (some new retrieval cue) with what you learned – maybe the smell of coffee, the sight of leaves, even a feeling of happiness that you get when you are outside. Or, in the case of movement or song or visualization, some particular movement, melody or image becomes linked to the lines you learned. In the audition, perhaps the director's coffee could then serve as the retrieval cue or just tapping your foot – if you learned a line while doing so, making it more likely you will remember your lines. The idea is that the more places and ways you practice things, the more cues you will have associated with that information, and the more cues you could use later when you have to recall it to get the info out. If you only learn in one way in one place, you only have the cues from that one form of learning to get it out later.

Sian Beilock

I was quite amazed at how easily the words came, and I was very aware that while I was teaching, I was seeing (if not concentrating on) the little pictures I had drawn. This success led to me to suggest to some of the performers that when they hit points where the words kept failing them, they draw a picture of the last word they could remember, next to a picture of the first word they forgot. It seemed to be extremely effective, particularly if the drawing was memorably silly: in the example above I can still vividly see the pictures I drew for fossils holding keys, spools, lightning bolts, etc.

Of course, we were learning under artificially pressured conditions, where we didn't have the time to learn at our leisure or in the way that most singers would prefer to learn. When we have the time, and under normal circumstances, it's much better for us to learn in rehearsal, slowly building up our knowledge of all of the actions and sequences of a given piece and then working through them and experimenting in rehearsal. But auditions aren't 'normal circumstances', and when it comes to learning material for auditions (where we are under far more pressure) it is important to be aware of how we remember initially and how we will be feeling when trying to recall this information under stress. For this reason, it may well be that pieces you learn for audition would benefit from starting out as visual memories before passing them through your usual memory processes.

EXERCISE FOUR

This is a challenging exercise that takes a couple of days to complete, but have patience – it just might surprise you.

I've found that this has different effects on different people. Some people I've worked with find it fairly easy to do and these same people seem to find it particularly helpful in remembering text. Some find it tougher and don't seem to connect with the visual images quite as easily. There is much research, however, that supports the idea that visualisation is a powerful part of memory. If you complete this you'll have a good sense of whether spending the time on creating visual memories will pay off for you.

Find a short part (about six lines) of a Shakespeare text that you don't know (Shakespeare tends to be a tough test of memory). Write or type it out with a good amount of space between the lines. In these spaces, create a visual image for each word or phrase. You don't necessarily have to draw exactly what each word is, since that would only be possible with certain words. For example, I took these lines:

The reason is your spirits are attentive/For do but note a wild and wanton herd/or race of youthful and unhandled colts/

fetching mad bounds, bellowing, neighing loud/which is the hot condition of their blood

I drew a raisin, some attentive ghosts, the number four, some 'Colt 45' guns, bellows, and so on. Sometimes the more bizarre the image (I drew a bowl of wonton soup for 'wanton'), the better I remembered it. It will take some time, and what you draw to represent abstract things will be personal to you. For example, for abstract words like 'fear' you might think about drawing something that you're frightened by – perhaps a spider?

Once you've finished your four to six lines with all the drawings, simply read the lines four or five times, looking at the drawings as you do. Don't do any of your usual text preparation or memorisation and don't make any effort to memorise or even analyse the text. Just read it through and look at the drawings as directed, then put it away for at least a day.

If, at any point during the day the 'word pictures' come back to you, try to remember what was near the 'word picture' that's just popped into your mind. You might find that some come to you very clearly. Unless you have a very busy, distracting day, it's likely that these 'word pictures' will come to you at least a couple of times. Just allow whatever you remember (without making too much effort) to come into your mind. The next day, read along with the pictures a few times, and after that keep the text covered and simply go through the pictures.

At this point most of the text should come to you simply by looking at the pictures. The more you can go through the picture sequence, recalling (but not reading) the text, the better. Do this a couple of times, three or four times on this second day, and then just put it away. On the third day, see what you can recall before you get the pictures/text out again. Then go through just the pictures again three or four times. By this time the words should come quite easily.

At points during the exercise you can start to think about the meaning of the words or what kinds of choices you want to make with this brief text as an actor. Although the point of this exercise is to test your visual recall, you will always want to engage your performance imagination when you learn text.

On the fourth day, see if you can recall the text without your notes or the drawings. Pay attention to how you recall the text (you may find at this point that it is a mixture of picture, feeling and text). If you remember the pictures prominently as you go though, you probably have good access to your visual memory. Because using the visual side of your brain when under pressure is preferable to using the language side, you will find it worth your while to learn audition material in this way.

The other thing that helped us during *Popstar to Operastar* was the music itself. Music is a perfect 'cognitive outsourcing' tool: it can aid memory, and also requires a number of different parts of the brain for its retrieval. It may be that, along with learning in a visual way, putting your text into song form could help you to learn it. I've found it to be particularly effective if I make up a tune that is fairly repetitive and then go to the trouble of recording it quickly on my mobile phone. If I then play it back a couple of times a day I find that it is even more effective for me than visual pictures. Partly this is because the tune pops into my head at moments without me thinking about it, which carries all the text with it. There is also evidence that involving things like smell, location and touch can aid text retrieval, and it may be worth your while experimenting with these ideas. Because memory is stored in so many varied locations in the brain, our aim should be to retrieve through any pathways that aren't going to compete for precious 'cognitive horsepower' with the language/reasoning centre.

It's clear that there's still much research to be done on this particular area of memory and performance, but if Beilock's research is right, learning in this way is bound to lessen the risk of choking and losing text under high-pressure conditions. Anything that can help us avoid that sudden 'blank' feeling has got to be beneficial for our confidence.

Other things to keep in mind when learning

The following things aren't particular to learning material for auditions, but they become even more critical when we're under the pressure of auditioning. The way that memory works is truly fascinating, and while there's much research that has gone some way toward helping us understand memory, there's still a long way to go. One of the things that we need to be aware of is that when we're laying down memory, we do it in a very complex way. As we considered earlier in Chapter 4, we remember things best when we're in the same location, or the same mental or physical state, that we were in when we laid down the memories. In other words, when we're memorising our scene or monologue we're not just remembering a piece of text. We're remembering where we were, how we felt, what we could see, hear, smell, touch or taste. Memory brings along all this 'bonus' information, and if this is the case then we can surely understand why it is *always a mistake* to memorise in a 'rote' way: by always working in the same place at the same time, or even in the same mood.

When you're learning, move: preferably in the way that you'll move when you perform. When you're learning, keep your imagination involved. If you're doing a scene with heightened emotion, you need to learn it in that state. If you don't, you're leaving out a significant part of what your mind needs to remember. There are good reasons why actors lose text if you give them a completely new direction in terms of what they're trying to do. If an actor playing Ophelia has been performing her scene with Hamlet with the intention of reminding him how desirable she is, and she is suddenly directed to play the scene with the intention of scaring the hell out of him, it is very likely that she will struggle to remember the text. If she has learned and rehearsed the scene with a table, two goblets and a box of 'remembrances' and you suddenly ask her to play it as if she is on a bus, sitting next to Hamlet, it is just as likely that she will struggle to retrieve text. Mental and physical states are part of what you're rehearsing and learning, and when you change them you are tossing a spanner into your memory's 'works'.

For this reason, while you absolutely *do* want to rehearse your audition material in just the right mental state, you *don't* want to tie yourself to any one physical environment. Work in different places, but always keep your imaginative state intact. You never know where you'll be auditioning, so don't get used to one place that you always work in.

Try to work under pressure if you can. This is tough to do, since performers don't tend to sit timed exams or sign up for time trials at the local athletics club. But along with forming a support group, think about other ways that you could do your material under pressure. Perhaps you can ask someone you respect to watch your audition monologue or song. You could also ask them to listen as you try to cold read something. From time to time you might want to try to fit a two-minute monologue into a minute (time it). Any time you can add a little pressure as you work, it will help you get better at taking stress in your stride.

Four new ways to think about risk

1. If there is no absolute right or wrong in art, what is risk? It's simply this: *risk is refusing to accept the most likely interpretation*. So whatever you do, learn to stop yourself at any point when you recognise that you're working with the most likely interpretation. Ultimately, it may be that the most likely interpretation is all there is, but don't accept it until you're sure of that. Be tireless in your search for alternative, different and creative interpretations.

2. How can anything securely connected to your heart and your imagination be 'wrong'? The greatest fear most actors have of making big, bold choices is that they'll come across as hammy or overacting. But before you decide to confine yourself to timid 'televisual' choices, ask yourself this: when have you *loved* watching actors make big, bold choices? My guess is that your answer will be something like 'When the actor making them truly believed them'. Remember that boldness has a magic of its own. The truth about bold acting is this: you can't make any choice that is 'too big' if that choice remains firmly connected to your heart and your sense of belief.

3. Always be aware of what gives you pleasure as a performer. What possible pleasure can there be in the likely interpretation? There may be some, of course, especially if

you've spent much time thinking of alternatives and concluding that the most likely interpretation is still the soundest. However, most performers will tell you that some of their greatest memories involve doing something really bold and risky on stage and watching how the energy of that boldness affected everyone around them.

4. Refuse to categorise, submit to logic or spend more time analysing than you spend *playing* when you're working on a role. Balance your time. Put logic in its place: it's definitely important, but it should never be the only approach. Recognise when you're jumping to conclusions. Always try to think in terms of opposites, it's a great starting point.

The interview

It may sound a bit strange, but I regularly advise performers to treat interviews the way they might treat 'speed-dating'. It might seem a bit far-fetched, but if you think about it, in both scenarios you're trying to impress in a very short space of time. And when you think about speed-dating, it also helps you to realise what kinds of things you *don't* want to hear.

So for a moment, just imagine that you are at a speed-dating table, sitting across from a stranger. Let's say that your first question is: Why do you want to date me? Now imagine the person across the table saying 'I can't imagine dating anyone else'. Okay, well, that might be true, but how would you react to that? For most people a statement like that would signal that there's something a little odd going on with this person – maybe they aren't getting out enough?

Let's say the second question is: Why is dating so important to you? Imagine the person across the table saying 'It's all I've ever seen myself doing. I love the feeling I get when I'm dating, I love feeling like people are watching me. I've always dreamed of being a famous "dater"'. Now you're getting *really* worried – this person just seems to be talking about themselves and what they want. How can that possibly be an ingredient for a fulfilling date where you're concerned?

Let's say your final question is: What attracts you to me? Imagine that they answer 'Well, nothing particular – I'm attracted to lots of people and I just love dating'. If you haven't felt a great relief when the time for your 'speed-date' is up I'd be surprised!

Now, considering that scenario, let's think about what it is that people might say in a speed-dating situation that *would* get your interest and might make you want to exchange phone numbers. Surely it would take someone who could convince you that they're truly interested in you and in showing you a good time. And it would probably be someone who seems intrinsically interesting to you. Depending on your preferences, you might like someone with a great sense of humour or a great interest in the arts or a passion for long country walks (these all seem to come up regularly when people talk about their ideal partner). Of course, auditioning isn't exactly like speed-dating, *but* you still want to get to the point where you're meta-phorically exchanging phone numbers and you won't do that by going on about yourself endlessly. Nor will you do that by having nothing interesting to say about your passions, what makes you curious in life, what you read, what you watch, what you find fascinating, or by having nothing whatever to say about the person who's interviewing you.

In a way, as long as you work in the performing arts, you're writing and rewriting your answers to questions like the speed-dating ones, and you need to put time into making sure that you don't fall into the trap of simply talking about yourself. You want to make sure that you can convince the panel about your passion for things, but don't make the mistake of thinking that your passions must all be to do with performing.

I can remember one young woman – who was clearly a 'borderline' for us – who, when we asked what she loved to do, began to describe her passion for making cakes. She described amazing cakes – a lemon drizzle, a gooey no-bake chocolate, a rum-soaked fig cake – all of which she had created the recipes for. She told us about the triumphs and failures of her trial-and-error methods, and by the time she finished everyone had fallen in love with her. Even though she didn't make it through the final round, everyone wanted to advance her to the next round simply because she captured the panel's interest with her love of baking which somehow seemed to translate to us as a love of life. She just seemed like the kind of person you want in a rehearsal room when things get tough. Never underestimate the importance of a panel's sense of what you'd be like in a tough working situation.

If you're dedicated to the performing arts and want to say it, don't just leave it there. Tell the panel why. Why do the performing arts matter (and don't limit this answer to a lengthy consideration of why they matter to *you*: think about the question in a larger sense). I sometimes share a couple of stories with people in audition workshops about moments that have really inspired me. Here is one example:

In Edinburgh a few years ago I was watching a young woman, completely coloured in silver (clothes, hands, face, etc.), being the statue of liberty. As I sat and watched, I wondered why she hadn't chosen green as her colour and casually considered that performers who do this 'frozen statue' work always remind me of rowers. Compared to other athletes, rowers don't exhibit much skill, but they do exhibit stamina. As I was thinking these things a group of rather unruly school kids approached with a teacher who was trying very hard to make one extremely shy girl turn around and look at the 'statue'. But she was terrified and hid in her teacher's cardigan.

As I watched them I became aware that they were all Down's Syndrome kids who must have come to the Royal Mile during the Festival for one of the shows aimed at younger audiences. The terrified young girl was finally persuaded to turn and look at the statue and she looked as if she might scream or run away. But just at that moment the statue 'came to life' and had a little silver glitter in one hand, which she sprinkled lightly over the terrified girl. I can't honestly or accurately describe the effect this had on the young girl but it was profound. She went, in that moment, from being absolutely terrified to being absolutely entranced. Her face broke into the most winning smile, and she stepped forward with an amazed look on her face, and I marvelled at how quickly she had been transported from terror to wonder. I realised at that moment that when it comes to performance – of whatever kind – you just never know when your work is going to make a little magic.

I think most people have moments in their lives, like this, when they realise the power of performance and the ways in which perform-ance is nearly always life-affirming, and holds a little magic. It is a way of reminding ourselves that the human community is always in need of each other: always in need of some communication and always the better for being able – even in the briefest moments – to see into each other's hearts. Perhaps when you're talking about why performing is important to you, you need to think about what really inspires you in terms of the *importance* of performing in the larger sense.

Remember that whenever you audition, research that you do on the project, the place, the director, the writer – whatever you can – will give you extra ammunition when talking with the panel. It's also likely to help keep you focused when your mind may wander into areas that aren't helpful: like replaying and criticising your last answer. Staying focused and in the present requires concentration, and having something to say about the project you're auditioning for isn't just good 'schmoozing' – it actually helps you focus.

Finally, if you take the exercises and the work in this book seriously you'll be well ahead of the game if you're asked in interview what you're working on at the moment. You'll be writing, you'll be acting, you'll be thinking and you'll be so fully engaged with the work that you'll have much to talk about that is positive and it will be clear that you aren't just sitting around hoping that the phone will ring. Like any other part of the audition, interviews take practice, so do some. Imagine tough questions, and enjoy answering them. Make this part of the skills practice you do every day.

Summary

Auditioning requires that we rethink a lot of our customary prepar-ation habits and that we make sure the ways in which we approach and learn are the very best ways to support performance under pres-sure. If you complete all the exercises in this chapter you're bound to have a good idea of how to plan your preparation for the best possible performance. We've looked at skill development, learning methods and working in riskier ways, and we need to take all three seriously if we're going to truly change and improve our performance in audition.

At this point you should know roughly where you are. You know that there are some interesting new ways for you to approach your weekly practice, which should include work on technical skills, text, imagination and creativity. You know that your goals for mastering your art are broad, flexible and beneficial, and therefore extremely positive. You might be feeling ready to get on with planning your practice, rehearsal or play routine, but you really need to complete the next section of the book before you do. This is because, along with all the things we've looked at, getting our 'mental game' in shape is critical to performance, and nowhere more so than in auditioning.

What we've been covering in this chapter concerns your assessment of your skills: both technical and imaginative. But before we sit down to pull together a real set of plans for your work, we have to spend time looking at how we can be developing our mental approach alongside of all this.

9 DEVELOPING YOUR MENTAL GAME

This section is going to build on the foundations of what we discovered in the first part of this 'Toolkit' section, and focus even more closely on how we raise our mental game for the actual audition performance. Understanding our values, knowing where we've been and where we're going are all important for your progress, but it still isn't enough. We need to start getting ourselves in the right, positive mental place for performing at the optimum level in auditions. Sports and business coaches know just how important this part of planning for success is, and yet acting books don't focus on the importance of preparing the actor's 'mental game'. We need to prepare carefully because we're not talking simply about preparing a 'winning audition game', we're also talking about having the things in place that will enable you to find, nurture and hang on to your motivation so that you can keep yourself going through all the ups and downs of this business.

Talking about having a 'winning mental strategy' is often foreign territory for performers, but if you've spent much time in the business or sports sections of bookstores you're probably familiar with the way that many of these titles seem to recognise the importance of mental strategy. They include books such as *In Pursuit of Excellence: How to Win in Sport and Life Through Mental Training* and *Developing Mental Toughness* or *Mindset: The New Psychology of Success*. On one level I suppose many people respond to these kinds of titles with some suspicion. As we've considered, the whole area of 'self-help' is one that people often view as filled with rather 'new-age' ideas about positive thought and self-hype. Certainly, we would never expect to see these kinds of titles in a bookstore's drama section. But I'm reasonably certain that if we had, we might have seen some difference in the way that actors prepare and motivate themselves.

Without going into an entire cultural history of the 'self-help' book, it's fair to say that what began with Norman Vincent Peale's *The Power of Positive Thinking* in 1952 – which encountered a thunderstorm of criticism from the mental-health community for its 'simplistic' idea that positive thinking could affect the outcome of things – has now been more or less reaffirmed by scientific researchers the world over. From studies that compare the difference in performance between athletes who prepare a positive mental image of success with those who don't, or compare the difference between students who read positive thoughts before taking an exam with those who read negative thoughts before taking an exam, research has proved over and over again that mental state has a powerful impact on performance.

However, the suspicions inculcated many years ago by those who find this idea just too simplistic remain. Surely, any closely scrutinised example of the human psyche and of how life works would suggest to us that this is complicated territory. The mind is complex. Society is complex. Succeeding is hard, and failing is harder. There's no point denying any of this. And yet, a number of research studies suggest that something as simple as the power of positive mental preparation cannot be denied. The idea is easy to understand, and it's true: thinking positively about the outcome of an event can affect that outcome, just as thinking negatively can also affect the outcome. Sometimes negative thoughts that aren't specifically connected with an event can have disastrous consequences. Recent research has shown that something as simple as telling a group of Caucasians about to take a maths test that Asians are better at maths results in demonstrably lower scores. Similar research has proved that telling women just before a maths test that men are better at maths produces the same negative effect. Researchers call this the 'stereotype threat'.[1]

This is a good example of why our mental game is so important to our audition career. It's also a good reason why, as actors, we should stop trying to cast ourselves too narrowly one way or the other. The 'stereotype threat' research showed that when Caucasian men cast themselves as 'less good at maths' than Asian men, their results were diminished. Of course when we're auditioning, we want to know our strengths, but we should also consider the things we've rejected in that analysis and at the very least adopt an open-minded attitude.

I remember in my very first year at the Central School of Speech and Drama having an afternoon of coaching with the third-year actors who were preparing their showcase material. A young man did a rather violent, thuggish monologue, and I asked him why he was drawn to the piece. 'I'll always be cast as the tough guy' was his reply. I asked him why he didn't think he would be the 'sexy guy' or the 'lead guy' and he said he wasn't handsome enough and that his whole appearance was too rough to think of himself that way. He's become incredibly successful these days playing a very tough cop on the BBC. He's not good-looking in a traditional, leading-man way, but the tougher and more objectionable his cop character is, the more people seem to find him sexy. I put his name into a Google search recently and found any number of critics struggling to describe his unusual magnetism: 'a retrosexual alpha-male with immense sex appeal'; 'his hard-to-fathom sex appeal ultimately shines through'; 'a sewer-rat with sex appeal'. They don't know what makes him sexy. He didn't know what made him sexy, and I can't say I did either. But as I watched him I couldn't help wondering why he just wanted to do thuggish, violent material for his showcase, because I was convinced that *he* knew there was something sexy about himself too, whatever he may have said to me. That always manifested itself when he approached a female character on stage in a kind of 'voracious predator' way. So it wasn't that he didn't know his likely casting – but he still knew how to seduce, and I think that's made all the difference in his career.

Okay, I can hear you saying that this is a huge contradiction: surely we should know our strengths – didn't we go through this in Part 1? My point is not to be *unaware* of your strengths. In the case of the young man above, he certainly knew how he was going to be cast. But he also worked slyly (whether consciously or unconsciously) against his type and that makes him fascinating. But as well as knowing your strengths, it's important to be open to all your other possibilities as well: it would be a shame to burden yourself with the 'stereotype threat' just because you know your strengths.

This is only a small example of how our thinking and preparation mentally affects every aspect of our career. We may already understand the importance of developing a robust mental attitude that remains positive in the face of a very competitive business, and we may be able to acknowledge that research has proven the benefits of positive thought, but how can we learn to think positively in a consistent way?

Graham Jones defines 'mental toughness' as a combination of four basic skills: keeping your head under stress; staying strong in your self-belief; making your motivation work for you; and maintaining your focus on the things that matter.[2] Regardless of how you might feel about the 'self-help' aspect, it's no doubt true that having the power to master these four abilities would significantly change the audition experience for most actors. But how do we get there? This chapter will look at two main areas in finding the kind of mental strength we need for battling our way through the world of auditioning: handling stress and staying motivated.

Finding audition 'perspective'

'Keeping your head under stress'

Well, I know what Jones means here: he is writing about keeping your head *while* under stress. What we need is the ability to keep our head *above* the stressful conditions of auditioning. We looked earlier at the ways in which we load the weight of expectancy onto the audition experience, and therefore load even more pressure onto the audition. The more pressure we load onto the experience, the greater the stress. So this is the point where we need to work closely on gaining some perspective and losing some of our metaphorical weight. We'll start by assessing just how much metaphorical weight we're carrying into the audition room now.

EXERCISE ONE

Keeping your last audition in mind, or perhaps a combination of audi-tions that you've had recently, please answer the following based on: 5 strongly agree; 4 agree; 3 neither agree nor disagree; 2 disagree; 1 strongly disagree. Don't be tempted to second-guess this, or to answer the way you think you should. Be absolutely honest with yourself.

1. Getting this job will make a big financial difference in my life ____
2. Getting this job will make me feel so much better about myself ____
3. If I get this job the first thing I will do is call my mother ____
4. If I get this job I'll feel better about seeing my friends ____
5. If I get this job I can finally show those people who doubted me that they were wrong ____
6. I'll be lucky to get this job – there are so many talented people out there ____
7. Getting this job will make all those years working at (fill in the blank) worth it ____
8. If I get this job it will prove that I've been making the right choices all along about being a performer ____
9. Getting this job means I am finally a success ____
10. Getting this job will change my life ____

Total: ____

Scoring:

If you scored between 40 and 50: you're carrying a massive amount of metaphorical weight into the audition room. That weight is creating tremendous pressure and therefore upping your stress levels to a point where it's going to be very difficult for you to cope.

If you scored between 30 and 40: you're probably carrying an amount of metaphorical weight that allows you to cope with the audition experience, but doesn't *help* you. There's certainly much room for improvement here.

If you scored between 20 and 30: you're carrying a relatively lighter load of expectation than most, but you could still work on sharpening your mental game.

If you scored between 10 and 20: you're in the optimal position to cope with auditions because the majority of pressure you will experience will come from external sources (more about internal/external pressures later in this chapter).

If your score was high you might be wondering how you could have scored a ten on this test. After all, whether voiced or not, aren't these kinds of statements pretty common? No doubt they are and I've heard them many times. But each statement here actually 'frames' the audition itself as something far too critical and far too important, thereby increasing our stress and setting the conditions for that stress to 'swamp' us and leave us feeling that we can't retrieve our text, we can't do what we rehearsed, we can't think of good answers in the interview, we can't respond as ourselves and we can't show the panel who we really are. As we know, under extreme stress brain-power is actually dampened down. What we want under high-stress situations is the maximum 'cognitive horsepower'. We want to be firing on all cylinders, ready to respond in quick, interesting or witty ways, ready to rely on the whole of our minds and our experience to cope well in the situation. However, in a study using a functional MRI scanner it was revealed that when the brain is under stress it simply doesn't work in the way that it usually does:

> Being under pressure alters how different areas of the brain communicate. In a nutshell, the prefrontal cortex works less well and decouples – or stops talking to – other brain areas that are also important for maximal cognitive horsepower. The brain generally works in concert, as a network. When a particular brain area stops communicating with other areas, this can have dire consequences for our thinking and memory capabilities . . . Fortunately, the brain seems able to rebound after the stress is gone . . . That may be one reason we seem to be able to come up with good one-liners or counterarguments . . . long after [a] stressful argument is over.[3]

We will probably all recognise this 'fuzzy-headed' feeling when under pressure, so knowing just why this occurs is helpful. It also points to the importance of working hard to keep self-imposed stress and expectation to a minimum. But how can we do this? On the simplest level, we can work toward making sure that when we walk into the audition room our answer to all the questions above is a '1'. That might seem nearly impossible to you at the point of reading this, but the goal of this book is to get you there. And if you *can* get to that '10'-point total you will begin to see things in a different light. Here are some sample answers that score a '1':

1. Getting this job will make a big financial difference in my life: *there are many things that can make a financial difference in my life. I could choose to take a different vocational path; I could become a paramedic or a merchant banker. But right now I'm working at acting and I do it because I'm passionate about it. I find other ways to pay the rent. I know very well that even if I get the job, the 'big financial difference' will not be permanent, so I don't ever focus on finance when I'm auditioning.*

2. Getting this job will make me feel so much better about myself: *I already feel good about myself. I never let an audition affect the way I feel about myself unless it's a successful one, and then I just recall the feelings that success brought about and use them to my advantage at every future audition.*

3. If I get this job the first thing I will do is call my mother: *there are a lot of good reasons to be in touch with my family, and I do it all the time. Whether or not I get this job will have no effect on something as important as my relationship with my family, or how often I get in touch with them.*

4. If I get this job I'll feel better about seeing my friends: *I already feel good about seeing my friends. They know how hard this business is and they respect the hard work and the passion I put into it. Whether or not I get this job will have no effect on something as important as my relationship with my friends.*

5. If I get this job I can finally show those people who doubted me that they were wrong: *how others feel about me is none of*

my business. My success or failure has nothing to do with others and all to do with me – my passion, my dedication, my choices and my hard work.

6. I'll be lucky to get this job – there are so many talented people out there: *there may always be people who are more talented than I am, but there will be very few who have worked as hard as I have or who feel as prepared as I do, and none who have my unique qualities.*

7. Getting this job will make all those years working at (fill in the blank) worth it: *this job has no relationship to the jobs I work to keep myself going while I pursue my dream. I am not in this for the quick fix. I am in this for the long haul and that requires dedication and sacrifice. I am happy to take that on (after all this is my choice) and working at jobs that aren't ideal is just part of that.*

8. If I get this job it will prove that I've been making the right choices all along about being a performer: *this job alone can never do that for me. Only I can decide if my choices have been right. I know what I am dedicated to and what I do and why I do it. No one job can ever prove the worth of my choices – only my own happiness and fulfilment in what I do can do that.*

9. Getting this job means I am finally a success: *I am already a success. I take myself seriously and I work tirelessly toward my goal. In making the choice to follow my heart and in being disciplined, hardworking, strong and positive, I'm already confident about who and what I am. That in itself gives me a natural advantage over many other people and makes me successful in anything I do.*

10. Getting this job will change my life: *this job does not have the power to change my life. Only I have the power to change my life. And I do that through my focus, my ability to follow my own plan for my chosen life and my desired achievements.*

I'm hoping that as you read these through you'll begin to recognise how important the mental game is when approaching the whole area of audition. As you read them, if you feel like you're a million miles away from really being able to say these things and believe them, then *go back and read them over and over again.* If you can learn to think like this, you will be in the optimum mental state, not only for auditioning, but for living happily with your choice to be a performer. If you feel like you can believe some, but not all, of it that is great and probably makes you even more aware of how important that belief is for you. Wherever you are on the spectrum, this chapter is all about getting you to the mental point where you can read the ten statements above, along with the italicised responses to them, and truly feel like you can believe them, because they are a true reflection of where you are at this point in your life.

The importance of being able to see yourself and your work as a constantly advancing, soul-nurturing adventure lies in more than just feeling good about things. It lies in the power we have in persuading ourselves to BE what we say we're going to be. Focusing on the positive and making sure that when you talk to others as well as yourself you continue to focus on the positive is a critical part of keeping your mental game sharp.

It's worth going back to read through these answers often – especially before and after auditions – and in recognising that what we do and what happens to us in our career is usually the result of some choice we've made. In the moments of feeling like life is something that just happens *to* us, it's critical to remember that we are in control of the choices we make, which means that we are in control of *a lot.* Gaining a little perspective on your audition experience is a significant part of losing that metaphorical weight and getting mentally 'fit'. One way to get that perspective is to look at the bigger picture. So – you need to create a bigger picture!

EXERCISE TWO

You'll need a blank piece of paper for this: at least A4 size (could even be poster size, depending on how long you've been auditioning and how much detail you want to add). In the far left corner (either top or bottom) put a dot and next to it the very first audition experience you can remember. In the far right corner put another dot and next to it put the very last audition you had. If it was a great audition, put the dot in the upper right corner. If not great, perhaps midway on the edge of the page, and if dreadful, put the dot in the lower right corner.

Now just freewheel and draw your journey between the first and last auditions on this blank page. Let the best ones be 'high points' in the journey and let the worst ones be 'low points' on your map. Put a name on each dot of the journey ('drama-school audition', etc.). Try to get as much as you can remember in there, even if the journey has to meander around the page. Once you're happy that you've got a reasonably good map of your audition 'journey', fill in the following and don't leave any blanks (it might help you to read the two sample responses below before you fill this in):

The high points in this journey are:

```
1.

2.

3.

4.
```

My overall destination is:

```



```

There were a few good things that came out of my 'low-point' auditions:

```
1.

2.

3.
```

What things do your low and high points have in common?

> 1.
>
> 2.
>
> 3.

What did all of this make you realise?

> 1.
>
> 2.
>
> 3.

To help you get a feel for this, here are two sample exercises filled in by some volunteers:

Sample one

The high points about this journey are:

> 1. *How much I've learned along the way*
> 2. *How much I value that learning and the people who've led me there*
> 3. *I've done a lot of work that I loved*
> 4. *I've kept going forward (most of the time!)*

My destination is:

> *A happy working life in the theatre.*

There were a few good things that came out of my 'low-point' auditions:

> 1. *I grew more interested in music and joined a band*
> 2. *I met more people outside of theatre*
> 3. *I discovered the joy of exercise*

What things do your low and high points have in common?

> 1. *They are all associated with working intensively on something I love*
> 2. *They all involved relationships, many of them supportive and positive*
> 3. *They were all the results of choices I've made in my life*

What did all of this make you realise?

> 1. *It made me think hard about what I value and about how much I've actually done*
> 2. *That I didn't put down the really crappy auditions because in retrospect they weren't important enough to include on this map*

Sample two
The high points about this journey are:

> 1. *Clustered mostly in the second half of the timeline (i.e they are more frequent toward the end)*
> 2. *In periods of my life when I have had more of them*
> 3. *Connected to improvisation as a part of the audition process*
> 4. *Auditions in which I have had fun*

My overall destination is:

> I've moved more and more away from acting in the last couple of years, making a living from writing, mainly journalistic, but now also branching out into the creative (I'm working on a novel at the moment). As I'm still registered with casting agencies, I still get the odd audition/ acting job without pursuing them actively. Although this means fewer opportunities, it's actually been quite nice to have the freedom to pick and choose much more. So my destination point is getting my novel published, and then writing another, and then another and to keep going until my fingers hurt so much that I can write no more.

There were a few good things that came out of my 'low-point' auditions:

> 1. Work (surprisingly)
> 2. Stepping out of my comfort zone and learning that it doesn't kill me, even if I get things horribly wrong
> 3. Learning that if I view the audition as a 'test' or if I want/need the part too much, I usually can't control my nerves enough to do a good job
> 4. Discovering that worrying about what they want, rather than trusting my own choices/instinct, is counterproductive

What things do your low and high points have in common?

> 1. To trust my instincts
> 2. To take risks (this is a good rule for life too I suppose, and writing actually). If you take a big risk, you may fall flat on your face, but it could also pay off (but at the very least, you will be remembered)
> 3. You don't know what's going to get you the job. What works in one situation may not work in the next

What did all of this make you realise?

> 1. *That there are so many things out of my control in the selection process that there's no point worrying about them. The best thing I can do is to go into an audition with no other expectations than to try to enjoy it*
> 2. *That I need to trust my instincts; they are usually pretty good. And if I get something wrong, it's ok. I'm human*

Hopefully this exercise will help you to recognise the truth that: *the audition is **not** the destination.* In fact, you might want to hang that on your wall. The audition (any audition) is only a small point in a big map. And as you see in the second sample answer above, sometimes the destination changes. You may think now that performing is all you want to do in life, and that will no doubt help create the mental strength you need. But every now and then it's important to take a step back and look at the bigger picture. Even the most important audition is no more than a stopping point along the way. There will be more. There will be good ones and bad ones and sometimes the good ones have things in common with the bad ones, but all of them help you learn and all of them propel you forward. As we've already seen in our earlier exercises, *none of our work on auditions is wasted* – we get lots of benefits in our lives as a result of working hard on what we love. And when we look at the big picture it helps us to keep any individual audition in perspective.

Types of pressure

Pressure can create stress. As we've seen, the more we load ourselves with expectations, and the more critical we think an audition is, the higher the pressure – and the higher the stress level we carry into it. That stress can have a serious effect on our mental response, but we need to remember that there are different kinds of pressure, and having some pressure is critical to our success.

We all know the kind of anticipation and love of a challenge that is good for us. This kind of external pressure can feel like 'good nerves': the ones that give your performance a lift, get you excited about the whole event, keep you focused and on your toes. 'Good' pressure is what makes the audition experience feel thrilling and like something out of the ordinary. Most actors know this 'good' pressure feeling when they're performing in a play. Unless we're really under-rehearsed or under-prepared, and as long as we're not suffering from a crippling kind of stage fright, most of us like the adrenaline that pumps through us just before we head out of that dark wing onto a stage flooded with light. It gives us a kind of energy that experienced actors learn to work with and channel to power their performance.

But we also know that there's another kind of pressure – and this one can reduce us to a gibbering wreck. The first step in creating a strategy for dealing with pressure and stress, is to identify what it is that you really fear, and the second is to identify the pressure points and then to analyse which elements are external and which are internal. Locating and thinking about these pressure points for every audition you are about to face is incredibly helpful. Why? Well, firstly because it turns out that identifying and then writing out your worries goes a long way toward coping with them. In her study on how the brain responds to high-stress situations, Beilock concludes that:

> Simply put, disclosure seems to be good for the body and for the mind. When university freshmen, for example, are asked to write about the stress of leaving home for the first time and going off to college, they report a decrease in their worries and intrusive thoughts. Writing about their worries also leads to improved working-memory over the course of the school year. Expressive writing reduces negative thinking, which frees up cognitive horsepower to tackle what comes your way.[4]

Studies by Beilock and others have concluded that simply by naming and writing down your worries about stressful situations goes a long way toward dampening your emotional responses to them. Perhaps, in a more common-sense way, we already realise that much of what frightens or stresses us gets processed in our brains in a fairly unarticulated way. Once we really articulate – once we really outline what's worrying us – we have the power to be very specific about how we're going to confront these worries, and we can stand up to the 'free floating anxiety' of unspecified fears. The final question in the exercise below may or may not be something you can answer, but give it a try. Humour has an extraordinary power to keep things in perspective.

EXERCISE THREE

Time to grab your notebook. Take time with this and write it out fully. It's worth thinking, as you write, that you are <u>writing this stuff out of your system</u>. It's also worth remembering that if you can articulate what you're afraid of, you can create and rehearse a mental strategy to cope with it. It takes practice and dedication but it can be done. Make sure you leave a lot of blank space after every answer you write out, because Exercise Four will require that you write a bit more under each of the answers below:

1. My biggest worry about auditioning is:

2. The worst experience I've had in auditioning was:

3. The worst thing that can happen in an audition is:

4. Look closely at your three answers and then answer this question: Can you see *anything* funny about these answers?

Here are some sample answers for this exercise from a volunteer:

1. My biggest worry about auditioning is:

As you have probably guessed: My nerves! I've always had bad nerves in 'test' situations, and it doesn't matter whether it's a maths test or driving test or an audition. If I have to be evaluated to 'pass' something, it gives me nerves. Just knowing I get nerves is often enough to give me nerves!

2. The worst experience I've had in auditioning was:

Doing an open audition for an audience full of casting directors and theatre directors. We could hear everyone's audition through the speakers in the waiting area and they were a pretty tough crowd to please. The girl in front of me did a comedy piece and didn't get a single laugh. By the time it was my turn, I could barely breathe. I must have got through it on some sort of autopilot, because I don't remember anything after walking on that stage.

3. The worst thing that can happen in an audition is:

> *Brain freezing and/or tongue going numb, and that the people auditioning you will remember you as a blabbering idiot forever.*

4. Look closely at your three answers and then answer this question: Can you see *anything* funny about these answers?

> *It's all pretty funny in hindsight, isn't it?*

EXERCISE FOUR

This is a follow-on to the exercise above. Take your four answers and respond to them in the most positive terms you can, or in terms of what you might learn if your greatest fears came true. Approach this as if you are standing outside of yourself, and thinking as positively as you can. Here are some sample responses to the volunteer's answers above:

1. My biggest worry about auditioning is:

> *As you have probably guessed: My nerves! I've always had bad nerves in 'test' situations, and it doesn't matter whether it's a maths test or driving test or an audition. If I have to be evaluated to 'pass' something, it gives me nerves. Just knowing I get nerves is often enough to give me nerves.*

But: why get nervous about being nervous? Why not learn to think of nerves as energy: I can use my nervous feeling as a kind of 'adrenaline shot' of performance energy. I always make sure that I do some centring before I walk into the room, and if the 'performance energy' feels too strong I take a deep breath and visualise. I know that the more I audition, the more control I will have over my 'performance energy', so there's no point worrying about it – I'll just learn from every experience and keep getting better.

2. The worst experience I've had in auditioning was:

> *Doing an open audition for an audience full of casting directors and theatre directors. We could hear everyone's audition through the speakers in the waiting area and they were a pretty tough crowd to please. The girl in front of me did a comedy piece and didn't get a single laugh. By the time it was my turn, I could barely breathe. I must have got through it on some sort of autopilot, because I don't remember anything after walking on that stage.*

But: why did I let someone else's experience bother me at all? The more I practice my focus, the better I get at just blocking this kind of stuff out. It was a good learning experience, though, and I've learned that being able to block out distractions is a really important audition skill.

3. The worst thing that can happen in an audition is:

> *Brain freezing and/or tongue going numb, and that the people auditioning you will remember you as a blabbering idiot forever.*

But: no one will remember one audition forever, and anyway, if they do it will only seem funny and not serious. It's a good lesson though, and it gives me something to think about when I start organising my pre-audition mental 'ritual'.

4. Look closely at your three answers and then answer this question: Can you see anything funny about these answers?

> *It's all pretty funny in hindsight, isn't it?*

But: if it's funny in hindsight, can't it be funny now? Not in a trivialising way, but just in the knowledge that every single actor – no matter how successful – will have some 'nightmare audition' stories. Getting it all wrong is part of growing: if I never get it wrong, how will I learn? So maybe it would be good to remember the humour as I walk *into* the room, instead of after?

Your turn now: go back to your answers for Exercise Three and fill in your positive responses to them.

When we know we're about to audition, most people experience a combination of excitement and stress. The excitement is a good thing, but stress is destructive. This means that a big part of getting ourselves mentally prepared for giving the best possible performance in audition is to make that sure we've analysed and dismantled some of the pressure, stress and nerves of auditioning. By recognising which pressures are external and which are internal, we can get ourselves into a position where we can take control. As we outlined above, we know that there is a difference between internal and external pressures, so let's imagine a scenario and try to identify these different forms of pressure.

Let's imagine you're auditioning for a place at drama school (I'm hoping that this is a good general example, since some of you may be about to face this and many of you will remember it). You have been sent a full description of what the day will look like (usually one Shakespeare, one modern speech, an interview and/or a workshop). So where will the pressure (both before and on the day) come from and what kind of pressure is it likely to be? I would say that the following can all be starting points for pressure/stress:

1. I must learn two new speeches and do them well
2. I must anticipate that they'll ask tough questions and that the workshop may be difficult
3. I must compete with hundreds of other hopefuls
4. I must control my nerves
5. I must be able to relax enough to really show them what I can do

6. This is my second attempt at this place – I hope they do/ don't remember me
7. I just bombed at my last audition
8. This audition is critical for me – if I don't get offered this place, I don't know what I'm going to do.

So, which of these pressures are external and which of these are internal? More importantly, *why* does that matter? Well, external pressures come about when there are circumstances that you didn't choose. When pressures are external, there's not a lot you can do about them, except to accept them for what they are, find a good mental strategy for coping with them, and know that with each audition you will get better at handling them. But when pressures are internal then you must always keep in mind that *you have it in your power to change these or to get rid of them altogether.* Our next step is to analyse the pressure points we listed above quickly to see if they are external or internal.

1. **I must learn two new speeches and do them well**: you didn't choose this, so this is an external pressure. Often you won't get much time to learn the material you're asked to present, so this adds yet another external pressure.
2. **I must anticipate that they'll ask tough questions and that the workshop may be difficult**: you can't entirely predict what might be asked in an interview, nor can you know what might be done in an audition workshop. These aren't your choices, so these pressures are external.
3. **I must compete with hundreds of other hopefuls**: in your perfect world, you would be the only one auditioning on the day perhaps, or at least might not have to see the other auditionees. But in this situation, you are very likely to be thrown in with all the others and that can create an external pressure for you.
4. **I must control my nerves**: your sense of nervousness will depend on how you view the rest of the pressures, so some of this is in your control. This is both an external and an internal pressure.

5. **I must be able to relax enough to really show them what I can do**: again, your ability to relax enough will depend on how you view the rest of the pressures, and that means this is both internal and external as well.

6. **This is my second attempt at this place – I hope they do/ don't remember me**: this is entirely in your control. You have chosen to try auditioning here again, and that means that you knew when you made this choice that they might/might not remember you. This worry is not really connected to your audition, so this is entirely internal.

7. **I just bombed at my last audition**: this is a view that is coming from inside your head, and it is entirely within your control. This worry is not really connected to your audition, so this is entirely internal.

8. **This audition is critical for me – if I don't get offered this place, I don't know what I'm going to do**: your life is a series of decisions that you make, so knowing what you're going to do next is about how/what you decide. This worry is not connected to your audition, so this is entirely internal.

Now that we've analysed our list, we can see that what we have are three true external pressures, two partly external/partly internal pressures and three internal pressures. That means that we have the ability to eliminate (or nearly eliminate!) five out of the eight pressure points, simply by getting a grip on the internal pressure – the metaphorical weight – we're going to carry into the room. So let's get started.

EXERCISE FIVE

In this exercise, you're going to think of an audition that is coming up for which you can list all the pressure points you can think of (if you have no audition coming up, use your last audition and do the same). As you write these out, analyse which of these pressures are external and which of these pressures are internal.

Write out at least eight pressure points for an upcoming or recent audition (continue on a separate sheet if necessary):

1.

2.

3.

4.

5.

6.

7.

8.

Listing all the pressures/worries you can think of when you think of this audition, and trying to see which are internal and which are external, is your starting point. When you do this exercise don't censor your thoughts. Get them all down, because any that aren't here will continue to float in the miasma of your anxiety.

This list should now give you the ability to see what you can do something about, and what you can't do anything about. That knowledge alone is incredibly helpful, because in the swamp of nerves that can overtake us at times like these, knowing that you have some power is important.

The next step of this exercise is to create a positive mental response to each pressure, whether internal or external. So let's look at these pressure points again and start to build a mental strategy for coping. Here's a sample of some positive mental responses to our earlier 'drama-school audition':

1. I must learn two new speeches and do them well: *I can do this because I've done it many times before. This is what all my hard work has prepared me for, and because I have absolute confidence in my training and rehearsal approach, I thrive on this pressure. I have also spent time analysing how I learn best under pressure.*

and for me visual images (or it could be music, action, etc.), moving locations as I learn and performing for a critical friend are all useful strategies for me in preparing under pressure.

2. I must anticipate that they'll ask tough questions, and that the workshop may be difficult: *I can do this because I've spent hours thinking about why I do this, why I'm passionate about it, and on sharpening my skills. I've taken on advice about treating the interview like a 'speed-date' and I've been practising a lot. I've researched the school/director/project and that knowledge will help me as it gives me things to talk about besides myself. The unknowns are exciting to me, and because I train/rehearse in a dedicated and continual way, I will naturally be well ahead of my competition, so I thrive on this pressure.*

3. I must compete with hundreds of other hopefuls: *I don't worry about this. I don't compete with others – that is a waste of mental energy. I only compete with myself in terms of trying to get better in audition each time. Besides, having others around can be really supportive. My focus is on being prepared, responsive and on enjoying doing what I love.*

4. I must control my nerves: *I enjoy the rush of adrenaline I get when I'm about to perform – it's part of the reason I do this. And because my preparation is strong, I know that nervousness won't disturb me in audition – I think of it as performance energy.*

5. I must be able to relax enough to really show them what I can do: *I have some good techniques for relaxing when I perform and in situations like these I get the chance to use and test them 'under fire'. I am good at monitoring my responses under pressure and I know what I can do to lower tension when I'm working. This is all part of the hard work and preparation I've been doing for the last year, so this 'real' experience actually helps boost my ability to remain relaxed and focused while enjoying the adrenaline rush.*

6. This is my second attempt at this place – I hope they do/don't remember me: *It's great to be here this time feeling really confident instead of feeling worried. Whether they remember me or not is none of my business and it won't help me to know, because they might remember me for being good or they might*

remember me for being bad. Whatever memories they have, I will create a new impression today, so I don't focus on this worry at all.

7. I just bombed at my last audition: *What I did at my last audition is something I can't really know. I went through my 'post-audition' process,* I know exactly what I learned from that experience and I will put all of that learning into practice today. So I'm just focused on that.*

8. This audition is critical for me – if I don't get offered this place, I don't know what I'm going to do: *No audition is critical for me. I just don't think that way. There are things in my life that I dream of and I know that if I work hard and stay positive things that are right for me will come my way. I'm still in the process of learning and every audition offers me an opportunity to learn in leaps and bounds. I stay focused on the learning opportunities.*

Now, go back to your own list of pressures and create a positive mental response for each one, keeping very firmly in mind which are internal and which are external pressures. For the moment, imagine that you have been working through your skills development plan for about three months.

Write out at least eight positive mental responses to audition pressures (continue on a separate sheet if necessary):

1.
2.
3.
4.
5.
6.
7.
8.

---

* We'll be looking at 'post-audition' strategies later.

This part of the exercise may feel hard to imagine writing and believing at the moment, but be patient. As you progress with all the exercises in this book – both in terms of skills and mental preparation – you'll gradually become more confident about creating and believing these kinds of statements. You will no doubt begin to understand, however, that achieving this kind of mental toughness requires that you simultaneously work hard to achieve a level of mastery. In this sense, positive thinking and hard work create a 'virtuous circle': each reinforces the other and keeps you moving forward in the best possible way. You can and should use this exercise for every audition you do. It will really help your mental game.

Here are some particularly handy things to help you in writing out your positive mental responses to pressure. The first is to remember our mantra: *the audition is not the destination*. In this sense, we need to remember the importance of approaching our goals from an oblique angle. You need to keep 'reframing' the audition experience in your head so that you never see it as an end goal. Continually refresh your perception of it as a minor stop on a long journey, and you'll automatically take some of the weight out of it – and that reduces the pressure.

Reframing and obliquity go together. This is because once you reframe your idea of audition from 'I've got to get this part' to 'I love having the chance to show what I've been working on' (or something similar), you are coming at the goal of getting that part from a different, oblique angle, one that allows you to enjoy the journey for its own sake. If you can do that, you'll find a way of being at peace with one of the most difficult things about auditioning: getting rejected. We're going to get rejected and we have to be able to keep ourselves motivated, even when we sometimes lose.

The nature of an actor's life can sometimes be not working for months, and I don't think that necessarily happens because they're not training or they're not taking scene study class. Acting is a very difficult career choice.

I had an actor come in recently and read for an HBO pilot. He is a very good actor, but I could tell that he had lost his confidence. It broke my heart. I tried to give him a pep talk in the room, and later his manager called me. I said to him 'I'm glad you're calling me. I think that your client is a wonderful actor, and I hate to see his confidence so eroded. But he must know that not getting the job is not a reflection of his talent.' At some point you simply must make some kind of peace with the audition process, as difficult as that is.

Ellen Lewis

We can't approach auditioning head on, and we can't let rejection wipe us out. If we can learn to approach each audition as a side-stop on a great lifetime journey, we're on our way to 'making some kind of peace' with the hard reality of this business.

Remember that your focus always is on being the best you can be *at the given moment*. As circumstances change with each audition (maybe you have twenty-four hours to learn a song or maybe you had very little time to research the project), so your responses must be equally flexible. You can be the best you can be with twenty-four-hours' notice, but you can't be better than that. To expect more would simply add internal pressure – and our whole aim here is to lessen that pressure.

The audition routine

It's important that you learn to be disciplined and follow a routine in auditioning, but perhaps not for the reasons you think. Personally, I'm almost never drawn to the idea of routine: I tend to think that it's the enemy of creativity and play. But when we're talking about getting yourself into a positive mental space and staying there, routine and ritual are your friends. Part of what that routine is doing is helping you to practise your ability to stay in control of your own mental strength in the face of things (like auditions) that scare you.

There are a lot of different theories about how to handle fear and nerves, and as we've seen in the first part of the book, this is an area when our 'oblique' strategy-making comes into play. We know very well that we can't calm down by telling ourselves to calm down. We can't take it easy by reminding ourselves to take it easy. But we *can* redirect our focus, and when it comes to auditions there are two critical moments for that redirection. The first occurs in the 'anxious build-up' phase (roughly from the moment of getting an audition date/time) until you walk into the room, and the second occurs once you're in the room. These two critical moments require two different techniques, so let's take them in turn.

Pre-audition

The first area we're going to explore is an advanced combination of relaxation and visualisation. Neuro-linguistic Programmers call this 'anchoring', sports coaches often refer to this as 'centring', and some might think of it as being similar to post-hypnotic suggestion. Whatever you call the technique, it can be critical in terms of preparation. How you approach this exercise will be a personal thing. I find I have to mix things up in terms of trying to find the right way to get to the 'centre' of my practised relaxation mode. However, most people will tell you that this starts with the breath. The idea is to reach a level of mental focus where you can envision or feel the things that will get you feeling positive prior to the experience.

EXERCISE SIX

Anchoring

This is an adaptation of various exercises that I've found in different books, but the source of this 'anchoring' technique seems to be in Richard Bandler's early work in Neuro-linguistic Programming. I'm sure that this exercise is also related to various forms of meditation and self-hypnosis as well, so it is difficult to attribute a source. It's widely regarded as effective by a number of psychologists and researchers, and can be used in a variety of circumstances.

Think about a moment when you really enjoyed success. It could be a memory of coming out for a curtain call as the applause washed over you. It could be a memory of a phone call telling you that you got the part. It could be a moment when you received a reward or a scholarship. You're going to try and remember this moment in two ways. Firstly, simply write it down in a paragraph with as much detail as you can:

Here's my example: *I was driving home from work having just heard that my first book was going to be published. It was a warm summertime evening and I remember feeling almost giddy with excitement and couldn't believe that after all that speculative work I was really going to see my book in print. I can still remember feeling overwhelmed with happiness.*

Now write yours:

```



```

Along with the memory you've written out above, we need a 'clearing' or neutral image as well, so find something (I used a photo of my last holiday) that feels peaceful or neutral to you. You can either actually have this image in front of you or otherwise try to imagine it as clearly as possible.

Now we're going to take a moment to 'centre' and then see if there's anything to add to the memory, before going on to physically 'anchor' the memory. Read this through first before giving it a try.

Sitting comfortably in a quiet place, simply breathe very deeply and slowly into your stomach five times. Keep your focus entirely on your breath as you breathe in and out and allow that focus to distract you from thinking about anything else. On the fifth breath, roll your eyes upward to a comfortable upward position and stare at a spot on the ceiling or high on a wall. Breathe deeply two more times as you look up and then close your eyes. Breathe three more times, always keeping your focus on your breath (you're breathing ten times in total). We'll call this our 'centred' state. *If you find your mind wandering at all (which it probably will) remember to just bring your focus back to your breath.*

Now go back to your memory of a successful moment. Try to experience it completely. Go through all of your senses: sight, sound, touch, taste, smell. The chances are that you will remember more about it, but the most important thing is that you try to capture the true feeling of happiness that you felt in that moment. Once you feel as if you're recalling the strongest emotional sensation of that moment (it should be a combination of exhilaration and confidence), perform a decisive physical action (this could be pressing your hand against your chest, squeezing your hands together or pressing your thumb and index fingers together firmly).

Now that you've done this, focus on your 'clearing' or neutral image. The heightened emotion should subside and you should feel yourself feeling calm or peaceful. 'Breathe into' that calmness for a couple of breaths, try to keep envisioning your neutral image. When you feel really relaxed, envision and feel your state of success once again. Let this memory build until you think you're back in the highest emotional state (exhilaration and confidence) that you felt at the time and once again perform your decisive physical action. Cycle through these alternating 'success' and 'clearing' states at least four or five times, each time making sure that you perform the same physical 'anchor' action at the height of the 'success' state.

According to Bandler you should only need to do this a few times before you are able to 'top up' when you need to, to keep the memory from fading. However, I found that I needed to do it *much* more, and I also found that I needed to 'help' the physical action trigger the emotional reaction by breathing deeply as I did it and willing myself to remember. In other words, it wasn't an 'automatic' trigger for me in the way I've heard it described, but I know that for many people it is. In either case – or wherever you fall on the spectrum – it's still a powerful tool for centring yourself and finding a calm and positive state.

We'll call this exercise our 'anchoring' exercise, using Richard Bandler's terminology. Anchoring is one powerful way to prepare yourself just before you audition. If this works for you, and you can bring back your 'peak' emotional experience with the physical anchoring technique, then you'll need to commit to practising it and making certain that you're able to do this even under pressure or when you're distracted with other things.

There is another technique that also uses the power of mental imagery, and it works by creating a combined memory. This has been called a number of different things by Neuro-linguistic Programming therapists, sports coaches and psychologists, but my favourite is Jason Selk's: he calls this the 'Personal Highlight Reel'. Selk's book, *10-Minute Toughness*, is filled with some very specific advice on creating the highlight reel, but he's not the only one who has promoted this technique. Don Greene, who wrote *Fight Your Fear and Win*, calls this 'mental rehearsal' and it's a popular technique in most 'inner game'-type books as well as most books on developing mental toughness.

The exercise is exactly what it sounds like, and it's all about creating, visualising, and playing over and over again in your head an imaginary film of you at your best. Selk recommends using some mental 'clips' of your best past performance and some mental 'clips' of an upcoming great performance. Greene suggests that you could also take real footage of yourself in a great performance and watch it often enough to 'run the film' in your mind in a very detailed way. This, of course, only works for past performances, and however you approach this you will want to spend some time on creating the most detailed 're-playable' mental images you can. It sounds disarmingly simple, but research shows that it is, in fact, incredibly effective.

EXERCISE SEVEN

Past performance 'showreel'

The first part of this exercise is just recording some memories, all of which are points in your performing career so far when you knew that you were performing at peak capacity. How will you know this? You might have a memory of the applause-level rising slightly as you came on for a curtain call. Perhaps you remember a particularly successful audition. Perhaps you remember some work in an acting or singing class that was lavishly praised. If you have only one really strong memory, then simply work on recalling the detail for that one memory. If you have many more, try to take just the top three 'peak performance' experiences. I found that this took some time because of the amount of detail I felt I needed with each one. In order to get the most out of this exercise, you should probably do this when you're sure you've got an uninterrupted hour or so.

Try to recall between one and three peak performing experiences. As you do so, recall exactly what you were doing and where. These should be brief, one-line descriptions (e.g. 'Curtain call for Sweeney Todd*').*

Write your one-line descriptions here:

> 1.
>
> 2.
>
> 3.

Now that we have our first description of these 'peak moments' we need to add as much detail as we can. Start by going through your ten-breath 'centring' exercise from above. Once you've done your breathing and you're feeling relaxed and calm, close your eyes and simply feel every detail that you can remember by mentally 'reliving' the experience. In other words: don't describe it, just get inside your body and try to remember exactly what it felt like. What were you wearing? Where were you? Who was with you? What could you see? What could you hear? What were you feeling? Just take your time with this and try to recall as much as you can. If you have two or three experiences, be sure you do this exercise for each one.

After each exercise, make some notes so that you don't confuse things. Your notes might look like this:

> Spring evening. Warm. Red corset, full skirt, and shoes too tight. Richard and John next to me. Very hot and slightly giddy. Richard beaming. Applause keeps rising and then standing ovation! Very loud, very strong. John smiling, we step forward.

Make your notes here for the three one-line descriptions above:

1.

2.

3.

Once you've finished all your notes for each experience, read through all of the instructions for the rest of this exercise before you proceed.

First, go back to your 'centring' exercise once again. Close your eyes, and this time imagine that you're in a cinema and that you can see yourself on the screen. Try to see yourself having the experiences that you just described/felt. Some people find this kind of mental imaging pretty hard, and some people don't find it difficult at all. If you can't see this very well, don't worry. Your memory of being 'inside' the experience is powerful too. In creating your 'positive showreel' you can just substitute the feeling of reliving the experience for the feeling of actually 'seeing' yourself having the experience in your mind's eye. However, research does suggest that mental imagery is important, so even if you can only remember one image strongly, use that and then stay with the positive sense of reliving your great experience from the inside. Now repeat this exercise for all three of your positive experiences. This will become your 'past' showreel.

Now we need to create the second half of the 'personal showreel'. This is simply something that you can imagine happening when your upcoming audition goes really well. You might imagine shaking hands with the panel and everybody is smiling at you. You might imagine getting the phone call that says you got the part, or you can imagine your name on a poster. *Whatever seems like the best mental image of your success in this audition is what you want to be seeing.* Make this image specific to *this* audition.

Once you have your specific image or images, go back into your 'centred state' and run those images through your mind as specifically as possible. Your aim, of course, is to put the past and the future 'showreel' images together. Once you have them you can't practise this too often, but at the very least you need to do them once a day.

I've used this technique with a lot of different things in my life, and I can say from personal experience that it is powerful and effective. Every time I've been dedicated about doing 'centred' meditation and visualisation every day for a span of time (a few months), I've found that what I was envisioning has actually come about – sometimes in surprising ways, and sometimes in exactly the way that I was envisioning it.

> I think routine is very important. Unfortunately, a lot of people try to use something like visualization just before the pressure is on – say, the day before the audition or the hour before the game, and to me it just doesn't make any sense to use any sort of preparation that way. To me it's like asking you to throw a pitch you've never worked on in practice. The amount of preparation and rehearsal it takes to get your visualization right is an important thing to be aware of. I always advise the people I work with to make sure that they have a routine in their heads that they're practicing all the time. Of course, visualization is an abstract thing, and it takes a lot of concentration. You shouldn't try to use it just on performance day or just on game day because if you do that, you're essentially trying to use tools that you haven't mastered yet. And that's not the right way to do anything – especially because in the fields we're talking about, such a high level of performance is expected these days. So mastering the whole mental routine is what gives you that edge.
>
> Jason Selk

One of these exercises is bound to have more resonance than the other, or perhaps a combination of both works for you? I prefer the 'showreel', but a lot of people like the quickness of the 'anchoring' technique. Whichever you chose, you need to make sure that you've got your pre-audition mental state ready, and you need to practise as often as you can in the lead up to your audition. Make sure that, if you can, you do one of these exercises just before you go into the room, or before you leave for the audition.

As we saw in the previous exercises, the ability to stay focused and to 'reframe' things (like reframing 'nerves' as 'performance energy' or reframing the actual audition as 'just one step along the way') is critical in taking the stress out of auditions. For this reason, a simple daily meditation routine can do wonders for you in the audition room. Not only is meditation a way of practising focus (and of getting you into a state where things don't distract you when you're performing, or about to perform – as we'll discuss below), it's also the way in which you can really give your positive mental imagery space and time.

During the audition

At this point we need to consider what's going on in our heads as we walk into the room. Of course, the focus of this book is *not* on the bleeding obvious: being on time, knowing your material, what to expect, etc. But the bleeding obvious is important and needs to be taken in. If you want more information on kinds of auditions, what they will require and what they will be like, do consult the books mentioned earlier, which are incredibly helpful and full of sound information. As you might expect, the focus for us here is on how to cope with what goes on in your head as you audition.

So much of what goes on in your head will depend, critically, on how prepared you feel with your material and how disciplined you feel about your weekly work. As we've considered, once inside the room your main focus is to keep the 'mind flood' at bay – and that 'mind flood' consists of a number of things: thinking about things that don't need thinking about; carrying too much 'metaphorical weight'; reviewing ourselves as we go along; suffering 'involuntary' memories of past failures, etc.

Assuming that you've been putting in the kind of hard work described, there's really only one solution for all of this: *never, ever lose your outward focus*. The minute your focus switches on to you, your feelings and what you're doing, you are bound to get swept away in the mind flood. And as we know, finding and maintaining that focus calls for a lot of hard work and practice. You have probably taken acting classes that include concentration exercises for practice, and you probably realise the importance of developing the habit of concentration. But as helpful as that concentration is when you're performing, it's even more critical when you're auditioning.

I've spent some time researching this and I think that there are really only two ways in which you can increase your ability to concentrate in a way that keeps distraction at bay. One is to meditate. If you've ever tried meditation you will know how difficult it can be at first. There's no great secret to meditation beyond being able to keep random thoughts at bay. But there are a host of terrific side-effects that come from meditating, and for the auditioning actor just having the experience and the ability to focus very specifically and limit or get rid of distraction altogether is a significant weapon against the 'mind flood'.

Along with the other dedicated visualisation we've looked at above, you also need to have an image of yourself doing what it is that makes you get better, and this is where I think daily meditation is so important. Meditation doesn't necessarily have to be long to be effective. Many people feel that even a concentrated ten-minute session will make a big difference in your ability to concentrate and keep yourself in a calmer mental state, as long as you can manage it daily. I wholeheartedly agree with that, and I've learned that it is particularly effective if you either start or finish your session by focusing on what you want to accomplish in the day ahead.

For example, you could simply sit up when you wake in the morning and do some deep breathing to get yourself into a centred state. You could then focus on seeing yourself accomplishing everything you need to do that day, and see it all happening very easily. The very act of visualising yourself working happily at accomplishing things is a great way to strengthen your resolve and to keep a positive picture of yourself in your mind. You don't need to work hard at this: simply see yourself happily accomplishing what you need to accomplish, and then spend ten minutes just concentrating on your breathing and trying to keep your mind still and clear. Alternatively, you can do this other way around: concentrate quietly, keeping your mind clear first, and then finish your session by seeing yourself accomplish everything you have to do today. The discipline of doing this will help you greatly when it comes to keeping your concentration in auditions.

The second great weapon is all to do with how you prepare your material in the first place, and how you control your focus in the room. Depending on your level of experience you will no doubt be familiar with the kinds of fundamental questions that most actors are expected to have answered when they're preparing and rehearsing material:

- Who are you talking to?
- What is your relationship?
- What do you want to get/what is your intention in this scene/ monologue/play?
- What's stopping you from getting it?
- What do you have to make the other person feel in order for them to give you what you want?

No matter what your experience, these are the fundamental questions that you must be able to answer whether you're doing a song, a prepared monologue, an improvisation or a cold reading. Don't even think about doing an audition piece if you haven't answered these questions. However, while they are great starting points, and an absolute requirement, they are still not enough in themselves to help you keep your focus while under the stress of auditioning. In order to do that you need much more detail. You need the kind of detail that will keep you mentally busy with the very act of keeping that detail alive.

This means that along with answering all of the questions above, and as well as learning and practising the actual text of whatever it is you're preparing, you must also learn and practise what you're seeing. My aim here is not to write an acting textbook: there are plenty of those around and lots of classes to attend. But when it comes to preparing thoroughly for audition – where we're facing much greater mental 'demons' – we need to prepare differently. We've already considered the fact that we need to *learn* the material differently, but what I'm suggesting here is that not only do we need to learn differently: we need to learn *more* than we usually do when we're playing a scene with another actor or performing with a company.

EXERCISE EIGHT

Don't try this exercise until you're really familiar with your material. Don't try it unless you have a couple of hours, as it takes some time and intense thought. Don't jump at 'the likely interpretation'.

Choose a monologue or song that you're working on. Starting just before you speak/sing, describe in your notebook:

1. *Everything that you can observe about the person you're talking to*
2. *Where they are, what they're wearing, what they're doing*
3. *What they've just done that makes you speak/sing*

   Now in two columns, describe what they're doing throughout the monologue/song, as you speak/sing.

This is a difficult exercise, as it requires much preparation and thought. Here is a sample, done for Benedick's monologue in Act II of *Much Ado about Nothing*. The left column is the actual monologue, the right is what I imagine is happening while I speak:

	I imagine seeing Claudio sitting in Don Pedro's drawing room in a ridiculous red doublet, his blonde hair falling over his brow, reading a book of love poetry with a simpering look on his face. Don Pedro is just behind Claudio, looking at me in an apologetic way. Claudio hears me approach and is about to read one of the poems to me, but I stop him.
I do much wonder that one man, seeing how much another man is a fool when he dedicates his behavior to love, will, after he hath laughed at such shallow follies in others, become the argument of his own scorn by falling in love!	

	Don Pedro looks down as he knows the truth of this but Claudio looks at me defiantly as I speak. I stare back defiantly at him until he drops his eyes to his book, which he closes.
And such a man is Claudio.	*Don Pedro looks to me and I speak to him.*
	Claudio gets up to pour himself a drink from Don Pedro's table. I speak to Don Pedro.
I have known when there was no music with him but the drum and the fife, and now had he rather hear the tabor and the pipe.	*He takes a drink, turns his back on me and refuses listen to me.*
	Don Pedro switches his focus between me and Claudio.
I have known when he would have walked ten mile afoot to see a good armour, and now will he lie ten nights awake carving the fashion of a new doublet.	
He was wont to speak plain and to the purpose, like an honest man and a soldier, and now is he turned orthography;	*I see the book of poetry he's left on the chair, and pick it up, leafing through it.*
	Claudio slams his drink down and walks out of the room. I call after him, trying to make him turn and fight or argue with me, but he storms off in his silly red outfit. I toss down the book in disgust.

His words are a very fantastical banquet, just so many strange dishes.	
	I turn back to Don Pedro, who smiles at me, as if he knows something I don't.
May I be so converted and see with these eyes? I cannot tell.	

Things to take note of in this exercise:

1. Benedick's monologue *is* a monologue, so obviously everything I've imagined seeing here doesn't really take place in the play. But someone watching this will simply see an actor engaged in a monologue who picks up a book part way through.

Lesson: never, ever do a monologue in which you are talking to yourself. Let Hamlet talk to his father's ghost. Let Isabella talk to God. Always find someone that your character is imagining they are speaking TO. I think this is important enough, whenever you're performing, but it's critical when you're auditioning.

2. There is more detail in the imagined description than there is text, so there is a lot to learn and rehearse. The exercise above is just in sketch form: in each subsequent rehearsal I will add more detail.

Lesson: always have a lot of well-rehearsed detail. This keeps your mind concentrated, keeps your focus outward, gives you something to stay engaged with and keeps the 'mind flood' at bay.

3. There is a kind of limitless possibility of imagined detail.

Lesson: great acting is incredibly detailed. Detail gives you something to hang onto, and it makes you explore deeply.

The Gunfighter's Dilemma

In the sample text preparation above, you'll notice that in the imagined scene it is the fact that Claudio is about to deliver a love poem that gives Benedick a strong impulse to speak. The thought of Claudio reading some insipid love poetry out loud is enough to make Benedick feel that he has to speak in order to shut Claudio up. Always make sure, when you're writing out your imaginary details, that you give yourself a good reason to speak, and make sure that it is powerful enough to make you feel that you *have* to speak. The reason for this is contained in a little mystery that some brain researchers have called 'The Gunfighter's Dilemma'.[5]

Let's imagine that you're on a dusty street in some godforsaken town in the Wild West. You're facing a gun-slinger of some repute and both of you are walking toward each other, hands hovering over the guns in your holsters. Do you want to shoot first or second? Well, if you're like most people you probably think that you want to shoot first. But in any number of research studies, it turns out that this isn't your best option. What you want to do is to shoot second. Although it might seem counterintuitive, shooting first relies on the conscious mind, whereas shooting second relies on a much faster, more accurate part of your brain – the amygdala. You will respond to the threat on your life with greater accuracy and speed if the other guy shoots first. However, if *you* shoot first you will be involving the reasoning/thinking part of the brain which, as we've seen, can interfere in our affairs at all the wrong moments.

In the split second that your foe goes for his gun, your amygdala instigates a chain reaction that bypasses your 'thinking brain' altogether. This is also related to the way in which a rabbit will often outrun a fox, even though the fox is bigger, has a longer stride, and usually the advantage of surprise. Yet the difference between the two is significant: the fox is running for his dinner but the rabbit is running for his life.

Although auditioning isn't precisely like a gunfight, I've always thought that the Gunfighter's Dilemma applies to the way in which actors plunge into their material. The number of times I have watched an actor struggle to 'centre' or find just the right moment to begin, or try frantically to retrieve text or memories just before starting is legion. When I'm watching this mental battle before me I always wish that the actor had just taken time to really see and hear what it is that they're about to react to in their monologue. Of course this only applies when you're in an audition that calls for prepared material. But making sure that you imagine the other character doing something that you must react to quickly helps to bring you right into the kind of energy and mental focus that you need.

Believe me, if you did no more than thoroughly prepare your audition pieces as you just did in Exercise Eight above, you would be well ahead of most of the auditioning people that I see. If you added a regular routine of meditation, you can be almost certain that your concentration would be strong enough to see you through your audition jitters.

Post-audition

Grab your journal. This is the point where you want to write. You want to record details like date, what the audition was for, what you did, and – if you know – who was on the panel. The important thing here is to keep everything in positive terms. It doesn't matter whether you got the job or not, just keep it positive. That doesn't mean you don't learn from any mistakes you might have made, it just means that you don't write about 'mistakes', *only what you learned*. After every audition you should use the experience to inform your next outing, so each entry should include:

1. Three positive things that happened in the audition

2. One thing (based on this audition) that I would like to focus on improving

3. One or two ideas about how I will go about implementing that improvement.

This might seem like a trivial thing to go through, but in fact it's a critical part of keeping your mental strategy strong and forward-looking. It means that you're sitting down and thinking through the whole of the audition experience as a learning experience. You're making yourself think of three positive things (even if the audition was a disaster, try to find three things!) that you can take away from the experience and frame in positive language.

Then you need to write about one thing that could be improved. Keep it at one if you can: there might be more, but choosing just one not only keeps you from dwelling on the negative aspects of the experience, but it also makes you feel like you can handle it. Most of us feel like we can make a big improvement on one thing. Likewise, most of us feel overwhelmed when we think we have to make a big improvement in *lots* of things. Once you've thought about it, and chosen your one thing to improve, write it out for yourself.

> *Just thinking about the audition and trying to reinterpret it in terms of what happened and how you might change something for the future should be beneficial. The key is to not just dwell on what you did wrong, but to think about it in terms of what specifically was less-than-optimal and what you would do differently the next time.*
>
> *And an added benefit of writing is that getting our worries down on paper (or our negative thoughts related to the audition) tends to make them less likely to pop up in the future.*
>
> *Sian Beilock*

Writing about this one 'less-than-optimal' element will also help you with your weekly, monthly and yearly goal-setting routine, so now write out a couple of ideas about how you're going improve on your one 'less-than-optimal' element. Here is an example:

Three positive things that happened in the audition:

> 1. *I really listened to the scene partner*
> 2. *The improv section went really well*
> 3. *My voice didn't seem forced*

One thing (based on this audition) that I would like to focus on improving:

> *I want to find a better way to deal with very technical dialogue so that it doesn't trip me up.*

One or two ideas about how I will go about that improvement:

> *I'm going to stop worrying about getting all the phrasing perfect – I'm going to remember that basically it's a first attempt. As long as I focus on what the scene is about and what I'm trying to achieve, the words should take care of themselves.*

Three positive things that happened in the audition:

> 1. *I belted a G at 10:30 am!*
> 2. *My first song got laughs/good reactions*
> 3. *I wore my great audition dress. I'm not going to lie. I get excited when I wear it*

One thing (based on this audition) that I would like to focus on improving:

> *I would like to be better at getting my personality in the room with me. I am a dynamic personality, which is a lot of who I am as a performer, but this doesn't always translate in the audition room.*

One or two ideas about how I will go about that improvement:

> *I'm going to work on relaxing just before I go into the room and forget about stuff out of my control. Next time I'm going to try doing something physical (maybe running in place, or jumping) before going in to the room, because I think it will relax me but also keep my energy alive and not allow my personality to seem 'beige'.*

The pre-, during- and post-audition routine is critical to getting yourself into the mental state that will enable you to take on the challenge of auditioning and imagine winning. It will give you what sports psychologists refer to as 'mental toughness'. This is partly because – in a world that can sometimes seem largely out of our control (they wanted someone taller, they needed a native accent, etc.) – these are the areas that *we can control*. Knowing that we have some control is vital to feeling like we can ultimately take on this challenge and win. That sounds like a sports coach talking and, in truth, it is. They're in the business of getting the best possible performance out of their athletes, and they know a thing or two about mental toughness under pressure and the part it plays in a great performance.

Find your motivational keys ...

Being highly motivated, when you think about it, is a slightly irrational state. One forgoes comfort now in order to work toward some bigger prospective benefit later on. It's not as simple as saying *I want X*. It's saying something far more complicated: *I want X later, so I better do Y like crazy right now*. We speak of motivation as if it's a rational assessment of cause and effect, but in fact it's closer to a bet, and a highly uncertain one at that. (What if the future benefits don't come?)"[6]

Motivation is a key issue. Being highly motivated is the only thing that will get you to put a practice routine in place, and then stick to it come what may. It's what makes runners get out of bed at 5 a.m. in the winter. It's what makes dancers put in hours and hours to perfect a pirouette. It's what keeps figure skaters going after they've fallen on their butt 20,000 times. But this kind of motivation isn't common and as Daniel Coyle points out, it's not a particularly natural place to be. It's also, as he so rightly observes, absolutely uncertain. Of course it is. We could practise our little cotton socks off for years and still find that we aren't making a living as actors. So how do we find this kind of motivation?

For Daniel H. Pink, a man who's spent a lot of time thinking about what drives us, the key lies in what he calls Type I behaviour. This kind of behaviour 'concerns itself less with the external rewards to which an activity leads and more with the inherent satisfaction of the activity itself'. Type I behaviour, he says, 'is made, not born'.[7] His study has concluded that there are three essential 'nutrients' on which Type I behaviour thrives: autonomy, mastery and purpose.[8] It isn't that Type Is aren't interested in money and recognition for what they do. But for these people, money or recognition is not the whole story. Make sure that when you're making a training plan you keep yourself focused on those three words: autonomy, mastery and purpose, and stay focused on the fact that *all three are in your control*.

As we know, when it comes to motivating ourselves much of this effort must be intrinsic: *you* must feel like performing is something you *need* to do; increasing your skills is something that you *want* to do. The fact is that no one can really inspire you to work hard: it's something that you must choose for yourself. However, if you can make that choice, then how and where you put your focus becomes all-important. Of course, we know that despite all the work we put into this we may still never hold that Oscar, but this kind of sober realism won't help us keep going when we're tired. What *will* help us is to know this: *that the hard work we're doing will result in something positive and real*.

When we're practising and getting better and beginning to see the results of all our hard work in terms of *real* confidence and increased skill, we have the great joy of knowing that even if we don't win 'the bet' (or the Oscar), at least we were wholeheartedly betting on ourselves. We believed in ourselves enough to *invest* in ourselves and – more importantly – we enjoyed the journey.

Come at it from a different angle

One of the important factors in staying motivated is to keep our focus on the journey. The practice that you do and the auditions that you undertake are all part of a life journey that will lead you to some fascinating places and give you the kind of confidence that will result in having a real advantage in an audition – and, I think, life in general. This is because when we really master something we learn that we can push ourselves hard and demand a lot of ourselves, and we begin to understand the rewards of discipline and hard work. That self-knowledge does a lot for our day-to-day self-respect. We grow more confident. We begin to feel okay about expressing a well-founded opinion. We know that when it comes to our art, the person we need to please most is ourselves. The discipline and the standards that we want to achieve are the ones we've set for ourselves.

We've spent some time in the exercises in previous chapters trying to keep auditions in perspective, to see our work as *always having value,* whatever the audition outcome is, and to consider all of that within the context of a greater journey. In his book *Obliquity,* John Kay refers repeatedly to the importance of focusing on the journey rather than the outcome in terms of maintaining motivation. He believes that we achieve what we want to achieve best by coming at it indirectly. That is to say, we rarely achieve happiness by focusing on happiness. We achieve happiness in an indirect way: by focusing on doing what makes us happy. But he's also very clear that the indirect, the meandering, and the zig-zag approach has appeal in its own right, and is the only way to achieve our high-level goals:

> Obliquity is a process of experiment and discovery. Successes and failure and the expansion of knowledge lead to reassessment of our objectives and goals and the actions that result.[9]

His clear suggestion is that, although we have a goal in mind, we focus on the journey: constantly adapting, changing and rethinking as we go, because in this way we're likely either to reach the original high-level goal we set or to find that we've achieved something else entirely, that we're equally happy with.

It's especially important that we learn to come at our desire to be a successful performer in terms of a journey, and to remember that *the audition is not the destination*. In truth, of course, even a wildly successful audition isn't an outcome, it's a signpost on the journey: a nice, positive one, saying that you're heading in the right direction.

The question for the dedicated performer, then, is this: What *is* my outcome? Perhaps the most widely acceptable answer to that question is: 'I want to be the best. I want to create work that is acknowledged to be of the very best standard I can possibly produce. I want to be recognised by people I respect as being the very best at what I do'.

But what do we want to be the best *for*?

Link your motivation to a higher purpose

It's a fact. Linking your motivation to a higher power makes a difference in the quality of the outcome. Athletes have proved this over and over again, and many research studies have shown that when we think we're working for something greater than ourselves we gain an extra boost. It's common sense really, and for Matthew Syed this kind of 'higher-purpose' belief forms part of what he calls the Placebo Effect. Syed writes specifically about the great triple-jump athlete Jonathan Edwards, whose spiritual commitment when he was competing meant that he always thought his athletic achievement was dedicated to something higher than his own ego gain.

In the earlier Exercises we looked closely at what we really value and what is important to us. If there's anything there that you feel you can link your work to – just do it! It can really help you in those moments when you feel your commitment wavering. Remember that it's easy to give up on ourselves, especially when times get tough. But it's not so easy to give up on something that we truly value, or truly believe in, or that gives importance to our work. Before you get stuck into creating your training plan, have a little contemplation time about this. *Why* is it important for you to be dedicated and disciplined about what you do and *how* can you benefit someone or something greater than yourself? When you're busy developing your skills and your mental strength, make sure you're always aware of what or who you're doing this *for*.

Summary

This chapter has been about wrestling as many elements of auditioning back into your control as you can. Combined with the previous chapters, you are probably feeling much more aware of why you perform, what kinds of approaches work best for preparing audition material, how to up the 'risk factor' in your work, how to shed some of the metaphorical weight that you carry into the audition, how to start really preparing your mental game for auditioning and how to keep your self-talk in positive mode, however things are going for you in the audition world. As important as all that is, I think the ways in which you talk to friends, family and colleagues about your work needs to stay just as positive. If you can learn to use the kind of positive language in Exercise One of this chapter whenever you're talking to others, you'll be gradually getting that kind of outlook fixed more firmly in your own mind. Your subconscious mind does listen to what your conscious mind says.

10 JUST DO IT

The Plan

Hopefully by this point you're ready to get started. Of course, if you've worked your way through everything in this book you've already started, and I hope you're feeling excited about the next step – which is to create a training plan that you can live with.

To be honest, this is the part of the book that makes me slightly nervous. This is because I happen to be very suspicious of people who tell me how to organise my time. So let me start by assuring you that no one is telling you *how* to organise your time here, but simply suggesting that you do. However, even this kind of advice can make me suspicious, and here's why.

I happen to think that a great many books that have been published on 'how to organise yourself' or 'how to make yourself more successful' or 'how to acquire the habits of highly successful people' are really a good idea. Once we're on our own, out in the world, we need this sort of thing from time to time. But too often we're not in a position to put the advice in place. They rarely start out by acknowledging that there is no single way to organise ourselves or to approach success. We have to find that for ourselves and unless we do find that for ourselves, we're not likely to stick with it. This means that we need to be able to observe and manage ourselves somehow (outside of the ordinary structures of our lives) and we need to be able to feel that we can shape our time in a positive and productive way – something that is much harder than most 'organise your life for success' books ever take into account.

But why is this so hard? Well, we begin our lives in such structured environments for so long (if you're like the average 'trained' actor you've spent more than fifteen years in a highly structured school environment of some kind for all of your formative years) that we find it difficult to suddenly be responsible for structuring our own lives and our free time. This why so many drama students I've known go through a depression once their training days finish: having to organise your own time can be a shock. Then there are some who have full-time jobs which already provide a lot of structure for their days.

The idea of completely rethinking our lives to accommodate extra hours of training might just feel too difficult for these people. If this is the case, then you know you aren't passionate enough to make the kind of commitment you need to, and that you will now have a lot to think about in terms of your future. But if you *are* passionate enough to commit yourself to mastering your art, then you probably want to be in complete control of how you do it.

When I was writing this section of the book I stumbled across a paragraph in *The Secrets of a Buccaneer-Scholar*, which somehow sums up what I feel about this section:

> School is temporary. Education is not. If you want to prosper in life: find something that fascinates you and jump all over it. Don't wait for someone to teach you; your enthusiasm will attract teachers to you. Don't worry about diplomas or degrees; just get so good that no one can ignore you.[1]

If, for you, performing is that thing that fascinates you, then now is the time to 'jump all over it'. You need to commit yourself to putting time into it, and how exactly you structure that time is completely up to you. Of course, for those of you who like a little help getting started, I thought it would be good to include a couple of detailed sample plans. These aren't so much for your use as they are to give you some templates to work from. The plan you make really needs to be one that makes sense for you and inspires you.

Some sample plans

Along with creating your own plan, it's important to have keep a journal devoted entirely to your weekly practice. Depending on how you like to see yourself working over time, you might want to think about setting daily, weekly, or monthly goals. I think I work best by keeping things on a slightly longer time scale, which allows me to take some 'side trips' when I get more or less interested in what I'm working on without worrying about whether I'm going to hit that goal or not.

However you want to plot out your work over time, start by deciding weekly, monthly and yearly goals and breaking those down into two areas: technical and creative. Technical goals tend to be related to voice (speaking, singing, dialects, sight-reading, handling heightened text, verse, etc.) or movement/physicality (fitness, working on 'neutral' physicality, freedom and ease, dance, tai chi, yoga, etc.). Always break goals into three further areas:

1. Overall yearly goals
2. Monthly process or 'step' goals that support the overall yearly goal and are concisely stated
3. Weekly objectives that are realistic and easily measured in terms of achievement

What you want to work on will depend on what you feel needs most work. You could start with Exercise Three in Chapter 8, and prioritise your work according to your answers there. However you structure your time, be sure that you're allotting at least half of it for work on the creative and imaginative areas. These are a bit tougher to write in terms of goals, but you can still plan. You have to be realistic about all of this or you'll end up feeling that you've failed – and that's exactly what you *don't* need. Remember that much of what you do in the creative/imaginative area can be worked into your daily routine in one way or another as long as you remain very conscious of what you're doing and why. In fact, the more you can work it into what you're already doing the better.

Start by considering how you use all of your 'unstructured' time: walking to the bus, riding into work, travelling anywhere, seeing a film or going to a gallery (remember the creative exercises we covered earlier), etc. Perhaps you can substitute some of your newspaper reading for reading other material more relevant to your needs. Going to the gym not only counts as part of your weekly ten to twelve hours, but it also gives you great thinking and imaginative time. Cardio work is boring if you're not distracting yourself with music or television, but research shows that when you *don't* distract yourself in these ways, cardio training has an incredibly positive effect on thought and inspiration.

Each of these samples follow the same structure and they build on the answers that you've come up with earlier in this book. The basic structure for your journal is:

Page One: List your top five priorities (this is here because keeping your values in your head at all times helps to link your goals to your values).

Page Two: What is your destination? (You covered this in Exercise Two in Chapter 9. This is here because it helps you to keep some perspective and allows you to be flexible in how you get to that destination).

The rest of the journal:
1. What are your overall technical goals for this year?
2. What steps are you taking this month/week to achieve your technical goals?
3. What are your overall creative/imaginative goals for this year?
4. What steps are you taking this month/week to achieve your creative/imaginative goals?

Make sure you leave a lot of room to write and reflect as you go through your year, and so that you can revise/adjust plans as you find you need to.

A Sample Ten-hours-per-week Plan

Achievable for someone working full time.

VOICE
Overall Goal for this Year: increase vocal strength and resonance, and clean up diction.

Monthly Goal: set a training routine and find a good book with exercises that I can follow.

Weekly Goal: 2 hours working through as much of David & Rebecca Carey's *The Vocal Arts Workbook* as I can, reading and focusing on diction exercises.

PHYSICALITY
Overall Goal for this Year: get fit and feel physically confident.

Monthly Goal: join a gym that I can afford and plan my schedule so that I can attend without too much difficulty. Try to talk with someone on staff at gym about setting up a good, progressive programme for my first month.

Weekly Goal: find and join a gym and make sure I spend at least ***2.5 hours*** there every week.

CONCENTRATION
Overall Goal for this Year: be completely in control of my mental approach.

Monthly Goal: research and practise methods of meditation and find one that suits me and start work on my 'personal highlight' visualisation and anchoring exercises.

Weekly Goal: one half-hour of meditation five days this week, practicing visualisation. ***2.5 hours.***

REPERTOIRE

Overall Goal for this Year: completely rethink and extend my portfolio, and significantly increase my cold-reading skills.

Monthly Goal: find and prepare two new monologues.

Weekly Goal: spend *3 hours* reading and searching for material.

TOTAL: 10 hours weekly

As you can see from this ten-hour plan, the time gets taken up quite easily. If you're working full time, it's best to start with ten hours and just see how it goes before you think of increasing your time.

A Sample Twelve-hours-per-week Plan

Achievable for someone working full time.

VOICE

Overall Goal for this Year: increase vocal strength and flexibility and be confident in my musical improv ability.

Monthly Goal: get *Vocal Workouts for the Contemporary Singer* by Anne Peckham and create an enjoyable vocal workout plan that I can follow daily.

Weekly Goal: spend ***2 hours*** singing along with some backing tracks, but make sure I *never* sing the melody as I go, but improv my way through. Record and check improvisation for accuracy, clarity and courage.

PHYSICALITY

Overall Goal for this Year: significantly increase my physical strength, stamina and flexibility.

Monthly Goal: increase the length of my cardio workout and experiment with new exercises (running, stationary or real cycling, rowing, elliptical, etc.); monitor and keep records of strength training and be disciplined about stretching.

Weekly Goal: make sure I spend at least ***3 hours*** at the gym this week.

CONCENTRATION

Overall Goal for this Year: be completely in control of my mental approach.

Monthly Goal: research and practise methods of meditation and find one that suits me. Start work on my 'personal highlight' visualisation and anchoring exercises. 'See' myself working on my weekly plan.

Weekly Goal: one half-hour of meditation five days this week, ten minutes of which are devoted to 'seeing' myself accomplish my daily tasks and twenty minutes of which are just concentrated stillness. *2.5 hours*.

CREATIVITY/IMAGINATION

Overall Goal for this Year: be in command of a variety of ways to put more risk, adventure and creativity into my work; to practise and master methods for avoiding the 'likely interpretation'; to be disciplined about writing and observing.

Monthly Goal: utilise all of my travel time to stretch my imagination.

Weekly Goal: I will devote my half-hour commute to work in the morning to observing, imagining and writing about people I see. *2.5 hours*.

REPERTOIRE

Overall Goal for this Year: completely rethink and extend my portfolio, and significantly increase my cold-reading skills.

Monthly Goal: find and prepare two new monologues or songs.

Weekly Goal: spend *2 hours* reading, listening, and searching for material.

TOTAL: 12 hours weekly

A Sample Fourteen-hours-per-week Plan

This is a lot tougher if you're working full time, but perfect if you're working part time.

VOICE
Overall Goal for this Year: increase vocal strength and flexibility and master two dialects.

Monthly Goal: find a good voice book and a good book on dialects and start to work my way through them.

Weekly Goal: spend *2 hours* working through as much of Barbara Houseman's *Finding Your Voice* as I can, reading and doing any exercises; spend *1 hour* working on exercises in Paul Meier's *Accents & Dialects for Stage and Screen*.

PHYSICALITY
Overall Goal for this Year: significantly increase my physical strength, stamina and flexibility.

Monthly Goal: increase the length of my cardio workout and experiment with new things (running, stationary or real cycling, rowing, elliptical, etc.); monitor and keep records of strength training and be disciplined about stretching.

Weekly Goal: make sure I spend at least *3 hours* at the gym this week.

CONCENTRATION
Overall Goal for this Year: be completely in control of my mental approach.

Monthly Goal: research and practise methods of meditation and find one that suits me; start work on my 'personal highlight' visualisation and anchoring exercises.

Weekly Goal: one half-hour of meditation six days this week. *3 hours*.

CREATIVITY/IMAGINATION
Overall Goal for this Year: be in command of a variety of ways to put more risk, adventure and creativity into my work; practise and master methods for avoiding the 'likely interpretation'; be disciplined about writing and observing.

Monthly Goal: visit at least two galleries, see one film and one live theatre event.

Weekly Goal: I will spend time observing and writing on what I see, and will also play with applying any observation to my own material. *3 hours*.

REPERTOIRE
Overall Goal for this Year: completely rethink and extend my portfolio, and significantly increase my cold-reading skills.

Monthly Goal: find and start work on one new monologue and one new song.

Weekly Goal: spend *1 hour* reading and searching for material; spend *1 hour* cold reading strange things!

TOTAL: 14 hours weekly

Making your own plan

Looking at these plans, you can see that they're pretty general: it's difficult to do a 'theoretical' plan like this because really they need to be tailored to an individual's exact needs. You will know exactly what excites you and what will be inspiring to work on. Overall, the plans probably don't look too taxing, but all change is hard, and if you're working at a demanding place in order to pay the rent, it is even harder. When reading these through you may realise that for you the secret is to replace some of your usual television-watching time with going to the gym, reading or rehearsing. If you can work your weekly goals into what you're already doing, you'll stand a better chance of achieving them.

In order to feel good about doing this, you have to do what you say you're going to do, so starting out by aiming to achieve ten hours per week is probably a wise idea. You will more than likely have weeks when that hourly number goes much higher. The important thing is to commit yourself to doing what you say you're going to do. You'll never get your mental game in shape if you can't remind yourself honestly that you've made a serious commitment to your career and that you're investing time and effort in yourself in order to get where you want to be.

Conclusion

As I write this conclusion, I've just finished a month-long, nation-wide audition tour for a new BBC show called *The Voice*. We saw some 20,000 people in six cities and I realised that I was right back where I'd started when I first began thinking about writing this book. And that, of course, brings us to the beginning: chasing the elusive 'it' factor in auditions.

Can we ever really know what makes up that intangible something that makes people behind an audition desk sit up and take note? I thought about this a lot while travelling through Britain looking for 'The Voice', and I still feel convinced about what I think invariably makes it up: a mastery, born of many, many hours of practice; a sense (for the auditioning panel) that you're in the presence of an artist; and a sense of real originality, either in terms of personality or new material, or a surprising take on extant material performed.

Of course talent plays a big part in this, but as we know vocal 'talent' in terms of the pop world can be a difficult thing to describe, especially when we consider artists like Leonard Cohen or Johnny Cash whose voices strike us first and foremost for being authentic enough to communicate some hard truths about life, however rough or scratchy they may sound.

During the auditions, we always interviewed the people who made it through to the second stage, and with the rare exception most of them had been working on their music – from training through to semi-professional or professional level – for about ten years, and many of them had been singing longer. That length of time invariably results in something that is difficult to describe as anything other than a very palpable and deep musicality. In most cases, this musicality was so assured that even when the singer occasionally drifted off into strange improvisational territory, you never felt worried about them or wondered whether they would find their way home – even through some very tricky harmonic structure. The sense of knowing who they were as artists was also usually present. In other words, they'd played long enough and in enough different places to know what worked for them and what didn't.

When I started out in the music business, older players always used to talk about 'paying your dues'. What they really meant was that in order to learn exactly how best to communicate your own feelings and thoughts, and your own sense of who you were as an artist, you had to play long enough and in a wide enough variety of places/styles to understand what it takes to communicate with people who may not have even come out to listen. You learn just what it is that an audience communicates back to you. It also means that, if you survive this long experience without becoming jaded or performing on 'autopilot', you begin to really understand who you are, what you can offer as an artist and what it takes to excite people with your work and your sound.

Perhaps the closest I can come to describing people who have that 'it' factor lies in one common element – whatever the material they are performing – which is that they understand absolutely that all great performance is based on a passionate and honestly felt need to communicate something. It isn't about demonstrating a great voice, it isn't about demonstrating that you can cry on cue. It isn't about hitting your high C faultlessly, and it isn't about doing a flawless triple pirouette. It's all about understanding why the crying, the high C or the pirouette must happen, must be executed with skill, just at that point, in order to truly communicate the piece. That's what mastery is all about: good artistic taste and judgement, the powerful employment of skill in the aid of communicating something, and in making us see the world in a new, perhaps unexpected way.

My whole purpose in writing this book has been to look at auditions in a different way. Partly this is in response to the many times that I've felt utterly baffled by the whole process of auditioning, and partly it has been because I truly hope that in looking closer at how we perform under pressure, and how we survive the tough life of being an auditioning performer, I might inspire people to take control of all the aspects of auditioning that they *can* control. I hope that it will prove helpful to my many colleagues behind casting tables up and down the land, most of whom are desperate to find prepared, focused and confident people who understand what it takes to audition with mastery and – if I dare say it – joy!

> You know, athletes talk a lot about having focus and they work at a fever pitch until they get to the big event and then they produce that focus and it's a joy, isn't it, when the 100 metres starts and they jump out of the blocks, very focused on the result. And because they've trained themselves to maintain that kind of concentration, they very rarely screw up. By and large it's a shame that you can't invite half a dozen actors in to watch the whole process for a day every time you do audition, because in a way I think it would help them if they had to see it from my point of view. If they did, they would see the terrible desperation of every single audition panel I've ever known to find good people.
>
> Trevor Jackson

I also hope that the idea of working toward mastery over ten years doesn't put people off the attempt to really get on top of what they love to do. It doesn't mean that you can't or shouldn't audition while you're in the process: indeed, auditioning is just one more training exercise and you learn from every one.

If I've learned anything in the many informal talks I've had with performers, and with people who cast them, while I've been working on this book, it's that when performers aren't being too optimistic they're being too pessimistic. I've done a number of informal surveys while writing this and I've been amazed at how hard some people can be on themselves and how negative some of their language is: 'I was lazy', 'I get arrogant', 'I have no confidence in myself', 'I just feel that everyone in the room is better' are just a few examples from the surveys I've collected. But these surveys didn't come from strangers – they came from people I know and respect, and whose talents I also know. Why do we tend to be so tough on ourselves?

I find myself going back to the article 'Unskilled and Unaware of It' that I wrote about in the first section and also, strangely enough, to a couple of lines from William Butler Yeats' *The Second Coming* (both of which seem to sum up so much of my experience when auditioning people): 'The best lack all conviction, while the worst/Are full of passionate intensity.' I don't mean to trivialise Yeats here, but his words are apt. Why are good performers so often dissatisfied with themselves and why are bad ones so often sure that they are great? Is it really so hard for performers to find a happy middle ground? Can we really not get to a place where we see what our strengths are and know how to continually work to improve where we need to? Can we not learn to see that there will always be some who are better and many who are worse, and that as long as we are able to keep our focus, discipline ourselves and dedicate our time to mastering the art we love, we will get to the point where we are 'so good that no one can ignore you'? Surely that kind of balance would give us a sense of ease about ourselves as performers.

I've come to think that so much of this negativity is really the result of the way in which we handle our fear and the way that we talk to ourselves. We're just not as good as we need to be in monitoring the ways in which we think and talk about our own performance. We probably know, instinctively, how important positive thought and language is, but we just don't seem to discipline ourselves in this respect. My research has led me to the conclusion that staying positive is critical. Like athletes and business managers, we're performing under pressure all the time, but perhaps the 'artistic' side of what we do has made people feel that talking about our work in terms of having, or not having, the mental toughness to survive it will somehow compromise that art. I believe that nothing could be further from the truth.

RESOURCES

Useful books

This is a brief section that includes books with practical exercises, interesting ideas or research that can help, guide and inspire your training plan. You'll find that each book will lead to others and slowly you'll be building your own library of inspirational sources.

Voice

Berry, Cicely, *Voice and the Actor*. London: John Wiley & Sons, 1991.

Berry, Cicely, *The Actor and the Text*. London: Virgin Books, 2000.

Berry, Cicely, *Your Voice and How to Use It*. London: Virgin Books, 2000.

Carey, David and Rebecca Carey, *The Vocal Arts Workbook and DVD: A Practical Course for Developing the Expressive Range of Your Voice*. London: Methuen, 2008.

Carey, David and Rebecca Carey, *The Verbal Arts Workbook: A Practical Course for Speaking Text*. Methuen, 2010.

Houseman, Barbara, *Finding Your Voice: A Complete Voice Training Manual for Actors*. London: Nick Hern Books, 2002.

Houseman, Barbara, *Tackling Text and Subtext: A Step-by-step Guide for Actors*. London: Nick Hern Books, 2002.

Rodenburg, Patsy, *The Right to Speak*. London: Methuen, 1992.

Turner, J. Clifford and Jane Boston, *Voice and Speech in the Theatre*. London: Methuen, 2007.

Work on dialects

Meier, Paul, *Accents & Dialects for Stage and Screen*. Lawrence, KS: Paul Meier Dialect Services, 2011.

For online resources with native speakers, the IDEA (International Dialects of English Archive) website has over 250 dialects and text samples: http://web.ku.edu/~idea/index.htm.

The BBC has an online accent and dialects archive: www.bbc.co.uk/voices/recordings/.

Movement

Callery, Dymphna, *Through the* Body. London: Nick Hern Books, 2001.

Dennis, Anne, *The Articulate Body*. London: Nick Hern Books, 2002.

Navarro, Joe and Marvin Karlins, *What Every Body Is Saying*. New York: HarperCollins, 2008.

Newlove, Jean, *Laban for Actors and Dancers: Putting Laban's Movement Theory into Practice – A Step-by-step Guide*. London: Nick Hern Books, 1993.

Pisk, Litz, *The Actor and His Body*. London: Virgin Books, 1974.

Potter, Nicole, *Movement for Actors*. New York: Allworth Press, 2002.

Acting

There are a lot of questionable contemporary acting books, so my advice would be to stick with the classics to begin with. You can always look further afield once you feel that you've worked your way through some of these:

Barton, John, *Playing Shakespeare*. London: Methuen, 2009.

Benedetti, Jean, *Stanislavski and the Actor: The Final Acting Lessons, 1935–38*. London: Methuen, 2008.

Boleslavsky, Richard, *Acting: The First Six Lessons*. New York: Theatre Arts Books, 1965.

Chekhov, Michael, *To the Actor*. New York: Harper & Row, 1953.

Chekhov, Michael, *On the Technique of Acting*. New York: Quill, 1991.

Hagen, Uta, *Respect for Acting*. New York: Wiley, 1973.

Meisner, Sanford, *On Acting*. New York: Vintage, 1987.

Merlin, Bella, *Beyond Stanislavsky*. London: NHB, 2001.

Merlin, Bella, *Complete Stanislavsky Toolkit*. London: NHB, 2007.

Stanislavski, Constantin, *An Actor's Handbook*. London: Methuen, 1990.

Stanislavski, Constantin, *My Life in Art*. London: Methuen, 1991.

Singing

Kayes, Gillyanne, *Singing and the Actor*. London: Methuen, 2004.

Peckham, Anne, *Vocal Workouts for the Contemporary Singer*. Boston, MA: Berklee Press, 2006.

Soto-Morettini, Donna, *Popular Singing*. London: A&C Black, 2006.

Meditation techniques

I find that everyone who meditates has a method they prefer. There many good online resources for this, so you can enjoy experimenting with some of these at no cost. That might be the best way to start, and once you've tried a few, you might be in a better position to invest in a book that looks appealing. If you're looking for some good meditation advice, these three books work well for me:

Fontana, David, *Learn to Meditate*. London: Duncan Baird Publishing, 2009.

Puddicombe, Andy, *Get Some Headspace: 10 Minutes Can Make All the Difference*. London: Hodder, 2011.

Ricard, Mathieu, *The Art of Meditation*. London: Atlantic Books, 2010.

Creativity, motivation, mental toughness and further research

Ariely, Dan, *The Upside of Irrationality*. London: HarperCollins, 2010.

Bach, James, *The Secrets of a Buccaneer-Scholar*. London: Simon & Schuster, 2009.

Bandler, Richard, *Make Your Life Great*. London: HarperElement, 2008.

Berns, Gregory, *Iconoclast*. Cambridge, MA: Harvard Business Press, 2010.

Beilock, Sian, *Choke*. New York: Simon & Schuster, 2010.

Carson, Shelley, *Your Creative Brain*. Cambridge, MA: Harvard Press, 2010.

Claxton, Guy, *Hare Brain, Tortoise Mind*. New Jersey: ECCO Press, 1997.

Claxton, Guy and Bill Lucas, *The Creative Thinking Plan*. London: BBC Active, 2007.

Colvin, Geoff, *Talent Is Overrated: What Really Separates World-Class Performers from Everybody Else*. London: Nicholas Brealey Publishing, 2008.

Corby, Larry and Jack Foster, *How to Get Ideas*. San Francisco: Berrett-Koehler Publishers, 1996.

Coyle, Daniel, *The Talent Code*. London: Random House, 2009.

Csikszentmihalyi, Mihalyi, *Flow: The Classic Work on How to Achieve Happiness*. London: Rider Press, 2002.

De Bono, Edward, *Lateral Thinking: A Textbook of Creativity*. London: Penguin, 1990.
Greene, Don, *Fight Your Fear and Win*. London: Vermillion, 2002.

Jones, Graham and Adrian Moorhouse, *Developing Mental Toughness*. Oxford: Spring Hill, 2008.

Kay, John, *Obliquity*. London: Profile Books, 2010.

Kelsey, Robert, *What's Stopping You?* Chichester: Capston, 2011.

Michalko, Michael, *Thinkertoys: A Handbook of Creative-thinking Techniques*. Berkeley: Ten Speed Press, 2006.

Selk, Jason, *10-Minute Toughness*. New York: MacGraw-Hill, 2009.

Zander, Rosamund and Benjamin, *The Art of Possibility: Transforming Personal and Professional Life*. Boston: Harvard Business School Press, 2000.

NOTES

Chapter 2

1   Berns, Gregory, *Iconoclast*. Boston, MA: Harvard Business Press, 2010, p. 121.
2   LeDoux, Joseph, *The Emotional Brain*. New York: Touchstone Books, 1998, p. 265.
3   I heartily recommend Margo Annett's *Actor's Guide to Auditions & Interviews*, London: A&C Black, 2004 and Richard Evans' *Auditions*, Abingdon: Routledge, 2010. They're comprehensive, extremely helpful and written by people who know what they're talking about.
4   Lakoff, George and Mark Johnson, *Philosophy in the Flesh*. New York: Basic Books, 1999, p. 10.
5   Wilson, Timothy D., *Strangers to Ourselves: Discovering the Adaptive Unconscious*. Cambridge, MA: Harvard University Press, 2002, p. 85.
6   Good sources for reading about these findings would include Dan Ariely's *Predictably Irrational*, London: HarperCollins, 2009, and Joseph Hallinan's *Errornomics*, Ebury Publishing, 2009.
7   See Fine, Cordelia, *A Mind of Its Own*. Cambridge: Icon Books, 2006.
8   Kruger, Justin and David Dunning, 'Unskilled and Unaware of It: How Difficulties in Recognizing One's Own Incompetence Lead to Inflated Self-Assessments', *Journal of Personality and Social Psychology*, Vol. 77, No. 6 (1999), pp. 1130–31.
9   Ibid., p. 1131.
10 Ariely, Dan, *The Upside of Irrationality*. London: HarperCollins Publishers, 2010, p. 94.
11 *Strangers to Ourselves*, p. 90.
12 Ariely, Dan, *The Upside of Irrationality*. London: HarperCollins, 2010, p. 272.
13 Apple, William, Lynn A. Streeter and Robert M. Krauss, 'Effects of Pitch and Speech Rate on Personal Attributions', *Journal of Personality and Social Psychology*, Vol. 37, No. 5 (May 1979), pp. 715–27.
14 Dutton, Kevin, *Flipnosis*. London: Arrow Books, 2011, p. 67.
15 Ibid., pp. 57–8.

Chapter 3

1   Damasio, Antonio, *Looking for Spinoza*. London: Vintage Books, 2004, p. 65.
2   See LeDoux, Joseph, *The Emotional Brain*. New York: Touchstone, 1998, p. 176.
3   Ibid., p. 148.

Chapter 4

[1] In a section titled: 'You're Nervous? We're All Nervous', Ginger Howard Friedman writes 'Incorporate your nervous condition into the scene. Give your nervousness to your character (read my book, *The Perfect Monologue*). *Casting Directors' Secrets*. New Jersey: Limelight, 2004, p. 112.

[2] Ibid., p. 42.

[3] Evans, Richard. *Auditions*. London: Routledge, 2009, p. 67.

[4] LeDoux, Joseph, *The Synaptic Self*. New York: Penguin, 2002, p. 222.

[5] Beilock, Sian, *Choke*. New York: Free Press, 2010, p. 147.

[6] Pink, Daniel H., *Drive: The Surprising Truth about What Motivates Us*. Edinburgh: Canongate, 2010, p. 109.

Chapter 5

[1] Syed, Matthew, *Bounce*. London: Fourth Estate, 2010, pp. 15–6.

[2] See Syed on Picasso, ibid., pp. 91–2.

[3] Colvin, Geoff, *Talent Is Overrated*. London: Penguin Books, 2008, p. 188.

[4] *Bounce*, p. 167.

[5] www.bls.gov/oco/ocos251.htm.

[6] Jones, Graham, "What Is This Thing Called Mental Toughness? An Investigation of Elite Performers" in *Journal of Applied Sport Psychology*, Vol. 14, Issue 3, 2002, pp. 208–9.

Chapter 6

[1] Kelsey, Robert, *What's Stopping You?* Chichester: Capstone Publishing, 2011, p. 17.

[2] Ibid., p. 17.

[3] Outlined in Kayes, D. Christopher, *Destructive Goal Pursuit*. London: Palgrave Macmillan, 2006, p. 36.

[4] Pink, Daniel H., *Drive: The Surprising Truth about What Motivates Us*. Edinburgh: Canongate, 2010, p. 59.

[5] Ariely, Dan. *The Upside of Irrationality*. London: HarperCollins, 2010, p. 31. Ariely relates the story of one poor volunteer to whom the prospect of the massive extra money was so great that he stole the money and ran away!

[6] *Drive*, p. 45.

[7] You can read about this study fully in *The Upside of Irrationality*. pp. 66–76.

[8] Footage available at: www.youtube.com/watch?v=I3YWszftWWg.

9 An interview with Csikszentmihalyi in *Wired* Magazine, September 2009, Issue 4.

10 *Drive*, p. 45.

11 Lazarus, Jeremy, *Ahead of the Game: How to Use Your Mind to Win in Sport*. Cornwall: Ecademy Press, 2006, p. 79.

12 Kay, John, *Obliquity.* London: Profile Books, 2010, p. 40.

13 Csikszentmihalyi, Mikhail, *Flow*. London: Random House, 2002, p. 218.

Chapter 7

1 Tharp, Twyla, *The Creative Habit*. New York: Simon & Schuster, 2003, p. 240.

2 Latham, Gary P. and Gary A. Yukl, 'A Review of Research on the Application of Goal Setting', *The Academy of Management Journal*, Vol. 18, No. 4, Dec. 1975, p. 824.

3 This is summarised from E. Locke and G. Latham. 'Building a Practically Useful Theory of Goal Setting and Task Motivation: A 35-year Odyssey', *American Psychologist*, Vol. 57, 2002, pp. 705–17.

4 Evans, Richard, *Auditions: A Practical Guide*. Abingdon: Routledge, 2010, p. 10.

5 We looked at this idea in Chapter 6 and if you want to read more fully about 'flow', I would recommend M. Czikszentmihalyi's *Creativity: Flow and Psychology of Discovery and Invention*. New York: HarperCollins, 1996.

6 Kayes, D. Christopher, *Destructive Goal Pursuit*. London: Palgrave Macmillan, 2006, p. 36.

7 Pink, Daniel H., *Drive: The Surprising Truth about What Motivates Us*. Edinburgh: Canongate, 2009, p. 133.

8 Kay, John, *Obliquity.* London: Profile Books, 2010, p. 14.

Chapter 8

1 I heard this story years ago and to be honest I have no idea where I heard it or who told it, but I want to thank whoever it was because it made me think long and hard about what I was doing as a young student taking acting classes. Its original source is equally puzzling, but I seem to recall that it was described to me as a Sufi story.

2 Berns, Gregory, *Iconoclast: A Neuroscientist Reveals How to Think Differently*. Boston, MA: Harvard Business Press, 2010, pp. 99–101.

3 Brown, Stuart, *Play*. New York: Avery Books, 2009, pp. 101–2.

4 Ibid., p. 37.

5 Ibid., p. 17.

6 Berns, Gregory, *Iconoclast*. Harvard Business School Publishing, 2010, p. 58.

[7] Bach, James, *The Secrets of a Buccaneer-Scholar*. London: Simon & Schuster, 2009, p. 168.

[8] Ibid., p. 171.

[9] Beilock, Sian, *Choke*. New York: Free Press, 2010, p. 130.

[10] Ibid., p. 131.

Chapter 9

[1] See Beilock, Sian, *Choke*. New York: Free Press, 2010, particularly pp. 103–5.

[2] Jones, Graham and Adrian Moorhouse, *Developing Mental Toughness*. Oxford: Spring Hill, 2008, p. 35.

[3] *Choke*, pp. 153–4.

[4] *Choke*, pp. 160–1.

[5] There have been a number of research studies that have borne out the truth of this, perhaps the earliest being one conducted by famous Danish physicist Niels Bohr.

[6] Coyle, Daniel, *The Talent Code*. London: Arrow Books, 2010, p. 106.

[7] Pink, Daniel H., *Drive*. Edinburgh: Canongate Books, 2010, pp. 77–8.

[8] Ibid., p. 80.

[9] Kay, John, *Obliquity*. London: Profile Books, 2010, p. 62.

Chapter 10

[1] Bach, James, *The Secrets of a Buccaneer-Scholar*. London: Simon & Schuster, 2009, p. 2.

INDEX